The Epistles of John

by Gerald Paden

SUNSET
INSTITUTE PRESS
3728 34th Street ◆ Lubbock, Texas ◆ 79410
1 (800) 687-2121 ◆ Email: extschool@sibi.cc

"The Epistles of John"
©Sunset Institute Press

This book is dedicated to my brothers:

Ivan, an elder
Cline and Harold, missionaries

for mentoring, role-modeling, and fulfilling
the Great Commission.

Special Acknowledgment

A special *"thank you"* to

W. R. Collier

who made the printing of this book possible.

Preface to the Sunset Bible Study Library

Since 1962 Sunset International Bible Institute has been a leader in teaching God's Word, training local church leaders and preparing preachers and missionaries for effective ministry. Developed in the laboratory of preacher training and proven in the crucible of practical ministry, the Sunset curriculum has grown to forty core courses used both in our resident school and distance learning applications. In 1989 the Sunset Video Studio was inaugurated to record each course of study in a professional format. Those courses, each with a companion study guide, have been used to teach thousands of individual students and develop a world-wide network of video satellite schools in local congregations and mission fields.

Now in printed form that same library of trusted Bible study material is available through Sunset Institute Press for an even wider circle of Bible students, thanks to a benevolent God, an excellent editorial staff and a number of faithful supporters who believed in the project.

This book is the result of a multi-step process which began with a videotaped course. The voice track of the videotape was first transcribed then formatted and edited from spoken to written style. The goal of the editorial process has been to produce a readable document while protecting the course content and the style and personality of the teacher. We believe the goal has been achieved and that each of the forty books planned for the Sunset Bible Study Library will likewise achieve that goal.

Special gratitude must be expressed to Cline Paden and Truman Scott who began the video course series in 1989, to Bob Martin, who directed Sunset Video Studio, to Virgil

Yocham and the staff of Sunset External Studies Division who wrote the study guides, and to the staff of Sunset Translation Center who edited the manuscripts and to each faculty member of Sunset International Bible Institute who took extra time to prepare and present these courses in the studio.

In addition to the English version, this book and its companion volumes are being translated into the major languages of the world to produce a Bible study library which can be used on the mission fields of the world to mature Christians, train church leaders and grow churches that plant other churches.

A companion workbook on the study of The Epistles of John by Gerald Paden is available for purchase through Sunset International Bible Institute External Studies: 1(800) 687-2121.

Table of Contents

Introduction
The Epistles of John

Welcome to the study of the Johanine Epistles. You will hear from the Apostle who writes as one who saw with his eyes, heard with his ears, felt with his hands, and contemplated with his mind the historical realities of the Messiah's mission and message. He writes as one of the apostles whose empirical experiences verify their collective testimony. The *"we," "us,"* and *"our"* of 1 John. 1:1-4 confirm the multiple, corroborating support for the message contained in this letter. In the verses cited the Apostle presents "his right to write." After all he lived through the history he records.

John writes as an Apostle who is an authentic interpreter of the life and teachings of Jesus. He is concerned about the doctrinal and moral soundness of the recipients of this correspondence. John addresses them as my *"little children," "beloved," "brethren,"* and *"the chosen lady and her children, whom I love in the truth"* (2 John 1:1). His concern grows out of the encroaching menace of error introduced by those whom he calls *"antichrist," "the deceivers,"* the *"liars,"* and the *"false prophets."* These *"spirits"* (cf. 1 John 4:1), as they call themselves, have penetrated the fellowship of the church with their insidious lies about Jesus' person and with perversions of Jesus' message.

It is obvious that John writes as one who deeply cares about the brethren and about the purity of the message they have embraced. Therefore, he writes as an apologist to defend Jesus' nature as to His deity, His humanity, and His messiahship. Frequently the Apostle becomes a polemicist —

one who attacks the errors that are threatening the doctrinal and moral purity of the church. John does not use the term Gnosticism. However, it is quite clear to scholars by his context that the Apostle is warning against and even denouncing and refuting several gnostic errors. Greater definition of those errors will be presented later in this introduction and particularly in the exegetical treatment of the verse by verse commentary on John's message.

The Theology of Assurance

It may appear strange to say, but thanks to the Gnostics, their errors have given rise to some of the most important doctrinal truths contained in the New Testament. The term "gnostic" or "gnosticism" is defined by the Greek word ***"gnosis"*** from which it is derived. Basically it means to **know** or **to have knowledge**. It will become evident that gnostic teachers placed exaggerated importance on a person's knowledge of their theologies and doctrines. It will be equally evident that John frequently employs gnostic terminology to denounce their subjective theories about God, Christ, morality, and ultimate salvation.

For example, some twenty-eight times John will say, *"we know"* certain things to be true. And ten times he will say, *"Hereby we know . . . "* and then proceeds to state the basis of the thing known.

So with strong affirmations, the inspired writer assures his readers of the reality of apostolic testimony. With the same solid convictions the Apostle strongly denies that Gnostics possess valid knowledge about Christ and the truths He taught. John assures his readers: *"We know that we have come to know him if we obey his commands. The man who says, 'I know him,' but does not do what he commands is a liar, and the truth is not in him"* (1 John 2:3-4). Such knowledge that is rooted in apostolic testimony contributes to moral self-discipline, to boldness in prayer, and to assurance of present and future salvation.

What Is the Christian's Source of Knowledge?

One of the greatest contributions the Epistles of John offers the believers is in the field of **epistemology**. This is a technical term that defines the basis or ground of knowledge. Epistemology answers the question of how one comes to know what he knows. It is a science that deals with the method by which knowledge is obtained. Knowledge can be purely speculative as John ascribes to the Gnostics, *"They are from the world and therefore speak from the viewpoint of the world, and the world listens to them"* (1 John 4:5). Or knowledge can be acquired by experience and by revelation (cf. 1 John 1:1-5). Proper biblical epistemology is crucial to the salvation of every person on earth. Eternal life for man is determined by the source and, therefore, the content of his faith, which is a by-product of his knowledge (cf. 1 John 5:13). John's teaching about the *"anointing"* (cf. 1 John 2:18-27) is a good example of epistemology.

John purposefully presents an apostolic epistemology. He says **they** bear witness to *"That which was from the beginning, which we heard, which we have seen with our eyes, which we have looked at and our hands have touched"* (1 John 1:1). He assures his readers that they are getting the same information the apostolic college received directly from Jesus during their three years association with Him. They saw His life and testified to it (cf. 1 John 1:2), heard His message and declared it (cf. 1 John 1:5), and wrote about what they received from Jesus. John said, *"Dear friends, I am not writing you a new command but an old one, which you have had since the beginning"* (1 John 2:7). The readers know that they are getting the same message the Apostles received directly from Christ: *"This is the message which we have heard from him and declare to you: . . . "* (1 John 1:5b). John is so insistent that his readers follow apostolic testimony and reject gnostic error that he emphatically states:

*We are from God, and whoever knows God listens to
us; but whoever is not from God does not listen to us.
This is how we recognize the Spirit of truth and the
spirit of falsehood* (1 John 4:6).

Clearly this is still a valid criterion by which to measure all
doctrine being taught even today.

Proving the Spirits

Many gnostic sects with all their different teachings pre-
existed Christianity. John affirms that there were *"many
antichrists"* existing in his day (cf. 1 John 2:18-19; 4:1).
Ecclesiastical history records at least four major contributors to
gnostic thought: Palestinian Judaism, Grecian philosophy,
Persian mysticism, and Oriental asceticism. Quite clearly each
contributor tried to syncretize Christianity along its theoretical
assumptions. **Syncretism** is an attempt to unite conflicting
beliefs and to wed theologies of diverse backgrounds and
ideologies into one common doctrinal package. The result
generally is the total perversion of the original truth being
taught by God's selected spokesmen. An example of
syncretism is presented in Paul's Epistle to the Galatians when
Judaizers attempted to mold Christian teachings along Jewish
doctrinal patterns. They tried to impose circumcision, Sabbath
observances, Hebrew kosher foods, and rituals and feast days
of the Law of Moses as essential parts of Christianity. Of
course, Paul rejected all such syncretistic thinking and efforts.
    Though gnostic philosophies of John's day were as
numerous as they were diverse, nevertheless, there was some
common ground occupied by all of them. They believed
matter is not only eternal, but it is also **fundamentally evil**.
Therefore, the physical body of mankind, being material, is
intrinsically wicked. Several errors were spawned out of such
thinking. Those errors in turn influence many other aspects of
biblical truth. The perversions that grew out of such thinking
contributed to confusion in each of the following areas:

theology, morality, Christology, anthropology, and salvation. John deals with each of these topics to expose the errors they contain and to defend relevant truth on each subject. Further explanation of each area will help understand the content of John's epistles.

The Origin of Dualism

The mystery religions of Persia contribute elaborate speculation about the nature of God. Zoroaster was a Persian "prophet," whose name has been given to a religion he founded some 600 years before Christ. His greatest contribution to Gnosticism was the formation of a rudimentary **dualism**. In his struggle to explain the evident contradictions in human experience, he developed the concept of two independent gods as the source of all creation, hence dualism in theology. One God was the creator of man's physical body and another God originated his soul or spirit. Dualism helped him explain the dichotomy (sharp division, Ed.) between good and evil, light and darkness, happiness and sorrow, life and death, health and sickness, etc.

Since the Creator God made man out of flawed matter, then man's body and bodily functions are basically evil creating a confused anthropology. That Creator God then must be identified with Jehovah of the Old Testament. He was the God of the flood, the extermination of Sodom and Gomorrah, and the God of the genocide of various nations in the Palestinian world. He was fundamentally evil.

Gnostic concepts about salvation are as novel as they are bizarre. Accordingly, Jesus did not come to save mankind from sin but from the prison of the physical body. Such thinking may explain Paul's reference to *"the worship of angels"* because they are pure spirit beings without physical bodies (cf. Col.2:18). Gnostic teachers assumed that the God who originated the spirit or soul of man is basically good and is, therefore, identified as the God of the New Testament. There was no open communication between the gods of the Old and

New Testament; they may have even been oblivious to the existence of one another.

The Beginning of Docetism

Gnostic prophets were forced to deny that Jesus was the Messiah of Old Testament predictions so they rejected His Hebrew roots. Further, their acceptance of dualistic theology made them loathe to believe that Jesus, who represented the good God, would voluntarily take on an evil physical body. Therefore, they developed the Christology of **docetism**. That term comes from the Greek word ***dokeo***, which means it only seems or appears to be. Several gnostic sects denied that Jesus had come in the flesh (cf.1 John 4:2; 2 John 7). They claimed that He only <u>seemed</u> to have a fleshly body; He did not leave footprints when He walked in the sand. Of course, such a phantom person could not be tempted with sin, could not shed redemptive blood, could not die a vicarious (something experienced through someone else, Ed.) death for mankind, and therefore, could not have been raised from the dead. It is understandable that John declares these men are *"false prophets"* and *"antichrists"* to be avoided with all caution (cf. 1 John 2:18-26; 2 John 7-8). Diotrephes was probably one of them (cf. 3 John 9). John gives personal testimony that negates their docetic assumptions. John states three times in his prologue that **they** saw, heard, touched, and contemplated Him as a real human being in a real fleshly body. Even in his gospel, John declares: *"The Word became flesh and made his dwelling among us. We have seen his glory, the glory of the One and Only, who came from the Father, full of grace and truth"* (John 1:14).

Errors about Sin and Morality

Perhaps the greatest confusion gnostic teachers created was in the field of morality and sin. The basic presupposition that matter is evil gave rise to **two opposite extremes** about morality. John takes both extremes to task. The **first extreme** fosters an antinomian attitude about sin. **Antinomianism** is a compound word that is best defined as *"lawlessness"* (1 John 3:4) The Greek phrase is ***hamartia estin he anomia."*** John used the verb of *"being"/estin* to define the nature of sin. Sin is ***anomia*** (***a*** = anti + ***nomos*** = law + is = ism). Lawlessness is the refusal to be governed by God's moral standards or laws. This extreme view holds that sin is merely a body function that does not affect the soul's relation with God. The Gnostic says sin is of interest only to the God that created the body. The God of the soul is not concerned with what the body does. Therefore, morality is a matter of total indifference to gnostic teachers.

Paul deals with some of the early expressions or manifestations of this thinking in 1 Corinthians 5:1-8 and 6:12-20. John deals with these distorted concepts in 1 John 1:6 and in Revelation 2:6, 14-15. John presents a caricature of a self-proclaimed *"prophetess,"* whom he calls *"Jezebel,"* for she and her cohorts boast of knowing the deep secrets of Satan (cf. Revelation 2:20-24). The Grecian Epicurean philosophies subscribed to such thinking with their proverb, "Eat, drink, be merry, for tomorrow you die." In other words, indulge the flesh without restraint because it will all be over tomorrow anyway.

The **second extreme** relates to the exact opposite result. Still based on the assumption that matter is evil, this view holds that the physical body is a seed-bed of evil deeds, and therefore, all passions and appetites must be suppressed. It developed into the practice of **asceticism** which insisted on the denial of even legitimate appetites. Such austerity resulted in the creation of monasticism, self-imposed privations, flagellation, and even mutilation of the body to promote supposed holiness through the suppression of desires.

The Greek Stoic philosophers insisted on stern self-denial as the road to spiritual virtue. Religions of oriental yoga and gurus were heavy contributors to asceticism. John denounces those who claim to have no sin or to have never sinned (cf. 1 John 1:8, 10). The Apostle Paul warned the brethren in

Colossae against *". . . hollow and deceptive philosophy, which depends on human tradition and the basic principles of this world rather than on Christ"* (Colossians 2:8). Many devoted to this extreme view separated themselves from secular society and lived in mountain-top monasteries and nunneries. There they practiced self-imposed denial which was articulated in the doctrines of *"Do not handle! Do not taste! Do not touch!"*(Colossians 2:21). Paul said,

> *Such regulations indeed have an appearance of wisdom, with their self-imposed worship, their false humility and their harsh treatment of the body, but they lack any value in restraining sensual indulgence* (Colossians 2:23).

Cold Intellectual Snobbery

Another significant gnostic view was the development of an intellectual snobbery about their supposed superior knowledge. Paul encouraged:

> *Timothy, guard what has been entrusted to your care* (the pure Gospel). *Turn away from godless chatter and then opposing ideas of what is falsely called knowledge, which some have professed and in so doing have wandered from the faith* (1 Timothy 6:20).

Such man-made doctrine and self-accredited knowledge is not knowledge after all! Apostolic truth should never be peddled for *"profane babblings"* (cf. 1 Timothy 6:20, ASV). John is quick to deny that the Gnostics have *"gnosis"* (knowledge). Yet their vaunted intellectual elitism created two classes of people. They viewed themselves to be the *"psuchoi"* (soul people) or *"pneumatoi"* (spirit people) as John uses their self designation in 1 John 4:1. All who rejected their philosophies were called the *"sarkoi"* (flesh people).

Gnostics claim to possess greater knowledge than the

Apostles. They considered themselves to be enlightened and to have been initiated into the understanding of the mysteries of life. They were intolerant of those who rejected their speculations. They were like the Pharisees, *". . . who were confident of their own righteousness and looked down on everybody else . . ."* (Luke18:9). The Pharisees derided those who rejected their traditions by saying, *"'. . . this mob knows nothing of the law — there is a curse on them'"* (John 7:49). The Gnostics of John's day had a pronounced hatred for Christians who were faithfully holding to apostolic testimony. This explains why they were so unloving and openly hostile toward the brethren (cf. 1 John 2:10; 3:10). Such animosity on their part gave John an opportunity to present some of the most fabulous lessons on love, which is such a prominent part of John's epistles.

Gnostics Were Not God's People

Without hesitation John assures the brethren the Gnostics were not a part of God's family. He said, *"They went out from us, but they did not really belong to us. . ."* (1 John 2:19). Because they hated the brethren, they were living in darkness and death (cf. 1 John 2:9; 3:14). They were practicing sin as *"children of the devil"* (1John 3:8-10). They denied the humanity of Jesus, His deity, and the fact that He is the Messiah (cf. I John 4:2; 5:10; 2:22). If Jesus were the Messiah, then the God of the Old Testament must be identified as the God of the New Testament also, and this was a concept the Gnostics disdained!

The Foundation of the New Birth

John presents **three major pillars** on which the new birth is founded. The first pillar is **moral** demanding a settled practice of righteousness — *"No one who is born of God will continue to sin"* (1 John 3:9). The second pillar is **fraternally social** because John uses *"love"* as a verb— *"Dear friends, let* *us love one another, for love comes from God. Everyone who loves has been born of God and knows God"* (1 John 4:7). The third pillar is **doctrinal** — *"Everyone who believes that Jesus is the Christ is born of God, and everyone who loves the father loves his child as well"* (1 John 5:1). The perfect tense verbs employed by John in each case are significant; they insist that whatever it takes to get the new birth is exactly what it takes to keep it!

Date and Recipients

The original verb tenses of 1 John 2:12-14 seem to relate to John's present correspondence (*"I write to you "* = present indicative) and then to refer back to previous writings (*"I have written"* = aorist indicative). The content of the former message seems to mesh better with his Revelation letter than with his Gospel. If that is true, then these epistles are probably the last portion of the New Testament to be composed. Most reliable scholars place the date of the epistles as very close to the end of the first century A.D.

Fellowship with One Another

So much of John's message has to do with the spiritual relationship between God and man that special attention must be given to it. Various terms or concepts are employed by the Apostle to give definition to the God/man communion. He wants his readers to share in a common fellowship *"with us,"* the Apostles, and *"with the Father and with his Son, Jesus Christ"* (1 John 1:2-3). Other phrases that suggest fellowship are: *"eternal life, which was with the Father"* (1 John 1:2), *"live in him"* (1 John 2:6; 3:6), *"remains in you . . . remain in him"* (1 John 2:27), *"continue in him"* (1 John 2:28), *"God lives in us"* (1 John 4:12), *"live in him, and he in them"* (1 John 3:24; 4:16), and *"We know that we live in him and he in us, because he has given us of his Spirit"* (1 John 4:13). Because of their presuppositions about matter being evil,

Gnostics denied the possibility of God having any kind of communion with fleshly man. Of course, John rejects their thesis and affirms the conditions upon which spiritual fellowship can be enjoyed by true believers. Therefore, 1 John can be outlined under the heading of fellowship between God and His people.

Fellowship with God Is Rooted In

Chapter 1:2-4   Apostolic witness of Christ's life.
Chapter 1:5-10   The moral nature of God — *"He is light."*
Chapter 2:1-2   The forensic advocacy of Jesus.
Chapter 2:3-6   Obedience to God's commandments.
Chapter 2:7-11   Keeping the new commandment of love.
Chapter 2:12-14   True knowledge about God and about Satan.
Chapter 2:15-17   The Christian's love for God.
Chapter 2:18-29   Apostolic epistemology.
Chapter 3:1-3   Understanding our status as children.
Chapter 3:4-10   Settled practice of righteousness.
Chapter 3:11-24   The practice of sacrificial love.
Chapter 4:1-6   The rejection of false doctrines.
Chapter 4:7-21   God's love perfected in practice.
Chapter 5:1-12   The new birth through true faith.
Chapter 5:13-17   Confidence in intercessory prayer.
Chapter 5:18-21   Assurance of Jesus' present ministry.

Due to the complex nature of the syntax of the verses in John's books, American Standard Version and New International Version translations will both be quoted in the verse by verse commentary.

The First Epistle of John

Introduction

In the first chapter, John discusses the issues relative to fellowship between the Creator and the creature. He affirms the reality of it, the immoral actions that preclude it, and the way the blood of Calvary establishes and maintains it.

The Prologue: 1 John 1:1-4

Fellowship is Rooted in Apostolic Witness to Jesus

That which was from the beginning, that which we have heard, that which we have seen with our eyes, that which we beheld, and our hands handled, concerning the word of life (1 John 1:1, ASV) [emphasis added]. *"That which was from the beginning, which we have heard, which we have seen with our eyes, which we have looked at and our hands have touched — this we proclaim concerning the Word of life* (1 John 1:1, NIV).

The syntax of the first four verses of this epistle is very complex. The first verse is introduced with the neuter relative pronoun, *"That"* (*ho*). It is then followed by four parenthetical clauses which explain the word *"that."* The neuter gender keeps *"that"* from referring to Jesus — at least initially. Jesus is not a *"that."* The *"that"* is *"concerning (peri) the word of life"* (cf. Acts 5:20) and therefore, it is the message about spiritual life. The *"life"* John discusses exists only when there is fellowship between God and man. A man can exist without fellowship with

God, but he cannot have *"life."* In 1 Timothy 5:6 Paul referred to a woman being *"dead even while she lives"* if she was living for pleasure only.

"From the beginning" (*ap' arches*) here is different than *"In the beginning"* (*en arche*) in John 1:1. Jesus pre-existed the *"beginning,"* in the phrase *"In the beginning"* from John 1:1. As the divine *"Logos/word,"* Jesus is not simply *"from"* the beginning. In 1 John the *"logos/word of life"* is co-existent with the *"beginning."* Hence, *"that"* refers to tahe *"word of life"* in verse one, *"life with the Father"* in verse two, and *"fellowship with the Father and the Son"* in verse three.

The *"beginning"* of John 1:1 and the *"beginning"* of 1 John 1:1 could easily be the same *"beginning"* as Genesis 1:1. In the Gospel of John Jesus is the theme, but in this epistle of John the **theme is *"life with the Father."*** That *"life"* is now made available through the message the Apostles heard from Jesus. If that is a proper view, then John here discusses the fellowship with the Father that Adam and Eve had *"from the beginning"* in the Garden of Eden. Certainly, Jesus also had fellowship with the Father and the Apostles confirmed the reality of its manifestation in what they personally saw, heard, felt, and contemplated.

"Since the beginning" in 1 John 2:7 probably relates to the *"beginning"* of the *"new commandment"* in its first declaration in John 13:34. *"From the beginning"* of 1 John 2:13 may refer to the knowledge that the *"fathers"* had about God at the time of their conversion. *"From the beginning"* of 1 John 2:24 is definitely tied to the earliest teaching the believers had *"heard"* about Jesus.

Fellowship Is With the Father

*And the life was **manifested**, and we have **seen**, and **bear witness**, and **declare** unto you the life, the eternal life, which was with the father, and was manifested unto us"* (1 John 1:2, ASV) [emphasis added]. *"The life **appeared**; we **have seen it** and **testify** to it, and we **proclaim** to you the eternal life, which was with the*

Father and has appeared to us (1 John 1:2, NIV)
[emphasis added].

There are three layers of **witness evidence** that John is
presenting to his readers. There was the *"manifestation"* of
fellowship between the Father and the Son making possible the
apostolic **observation** (*"seen"*) of it, followed by their
"declaration" of the relationship and its overarching implications
for believers. *"The eternal life, which was with the Father"* was
fully experienced by Adam and Eve in the Garden of Eden before
their fall. And that same *"eternal life with the Father"* was again
"manifested" in Jesus and *"witnessed"* by the Apostles during
their three year association with Him. For John, this *"life"*
principle was so personified in Jesus that His ministry and
message explained and demonstrated its authenticity. Jesus
exemplified the *"life"* so completely that He became the living
expression of it. The audible verbal interchange between the
Father and the Son confirms the Son's *"life with the Father."* The
Father's miraculous confirmation of the Son (cf. John 10:38; Acts
2:22; 10:38) gives further evidence of Their union. The frequent
affirmations by Jesus *"that the Father is in me, and I in the
Father"* (John 10:38 and cf. John 10:30; 14:9-11; 16:32; 17:21)
confirm that the Son manifested the *"life."* In Jesus the abstract
"life" took concrete form in everything the Apostles heard, saw,
touched, and contemplated/proclaimed through their sense
perceptions by which their observations were verified.
  "The life, the eternal life" (**ton zoen ton aionion**) does not
define the duration of life, but rather its quality. *"Eternal"* is an
adjective that modifies the noun *"life"* and defines the excellence
of the life and not its length. As to the quality of life, Jesus gives
"abundant/full" life (cf. John 10:10). The fellowship is so intense
that He promised: *"If anyone loves me, he will obey my teaching.
My Father will love him and we will come to him and make our
home **with** [Emphasis added] him"* (John 14:23). That is the best
explanation of *"the eternal life, which was with the Father"* as
John defines it. Christians have *"a new life"* (Romans 6:4); *"if*

anyone . . . opens the door, I will come in and eat with him and he with me" (Revelation 3:20). This is the believer's most treasured relationship, and it must be guarded with all diligence. John informs his readers that a man who has *"eternal life"* (cf. 1 John 5:13) may lose eternal life by *"sinning a sin unto death,"* (cf. 1 John 5:16, ASV). Only those who have *"life"* can commit a *"sin unto death."*

> *That which we have seen and heard declare we unto you also, that ye also may have fellowship with us: yea, and our fellowship is with the father, and with his son Jesus Christ"* (1 John 1:3, ASV). *"We proclaim to you what we have seen and heard, so that you also may have fellowship with us. And our fellowship is with the Father and with his Son, Jesus Christ* (1 John 1:3, NIV).

Jesus' *"life with the Father"* was a manifested reality for the Apostles. The *"message which we have heard from him"* gave the Apostles *"fellowship with the Father."* The same *"message"* is the vital link to the same kind of fellowship between God and any believer from John's time until the end of time. John *"declared"* the *"message to you so that ye <u>also</u> (hina kai) may have fellowship with us."* The word *"also"* defines the fellowship the Apostles had with the Father and the Son. Believers may enjoy the same fellowship that the Apostles had. Initially the fellowship is not horizontal, it is vertical. Horizontal fellowship between brethren can exist only when there is vertical relationship between God and His people.

John's **perfect tense verbs** are poignant because they define <u>past completed actions</u> that have <u>present continuing results</u>. Thus in effect, John says that they saw Him and His image is still seen in their mind's eye. They heard Him and His voice still rings in their ears. He was as real as the eyes with which they saw Him, the ears with which they heard Him, and the hands with which they touched Him. They *"beheld/looked at"* (**etheasametha** =

root word for theater) Jesus as if He were on a stage and the drama of fellowship between God and man unfolded before them during the earthly life of Jesus. *"And these things we write, that our joy may be made full"* (1 John 1:4, ASV). *"We write this to make our joy complete"* (1 John 1:4, NIV). The phrase *"These things"* includes all that John declares about life, about fellowship with the Father and the Son, and about collective apostolic experiences in their association with Jesus. John's concern is the present *"joy"* of his readers. Fellowship with the Father and Son is the relational root of joy for all Christians.

Some versions read *"your joy,"* but the proper translation is *"our joy"* rather than *"your."* In either case, John's joy is *"full"* only when his *"little children"* are faithfully holding to the truth (cf. 2 John 4; 3 John 4). His joy would be frustrated if they were to lose the full reward (cf. 2 John 8).

The phrase *"fellowship with the Father and the Son,"* easily translates into the present possession of *"eternal life"* (1 John 5:13). To know that Jesus *"remains in me and I in him"* (John 15:5) gives rise to His joy, *"I have told you this so that my joy may be in you and that your joy may be complete"* (John 15:11). There is too much joyless Christianity and that is an obvious contradiction of terms!

John exposes **five major gnostic errors** in the first four verses of 1 John. The Gnostics claim God will not fellowship fleshly beings because they believe matter is evil. For that reason the incarnation of Jesus just would not have happened. They also denied that Jesus was divine and that He was the Messiah. Contrary to their teachings, John affirmed that:

1) "Spirit God" had and continues to have fellowship with fleshly man.
2) Jesus really did *"come in the flesh"* (1 John 4:2; cf. John 1:14).
3) Physical bodies are not intrinsically evil because God fellowships man.
4) Jesus is *"the Son of God,"* and therefore Divine (cf. 1

John 1:3).

5) The term *"Christ"* affirms that Jesus is the long awaited *"Messiah"* of Old Testament prophecy (cf. John 1:41).

APPLICATION

Apostolic witness about Jesus and the benefits His mission of redemption brings to believers is as valid today as it was in New Testament times. Their written message carries the same authority as did their verbal teaching in the first century. It is still *"good news"* (gospel) to personally believe and to teach others. Christ offers us today the same fellowship on the same conditions announced by the Apostles almost twenty centuries ago. It is therefore urgent that we accept only what the New Testament Apostles and prophets wrote. Readers of this commentary should be alert to the dangers one faces when he listens to voices other than the original spokesmen chosen by Christ. John draws clear lines of demarcation between what the Apostles taught and what other pretenders to knowledge were teaching. Following Christ is still the only road to spiritual peace with God and joyful fellowship through Christ.

1 John 1:5-10

Fellowship is Rooted in God's Moral Nature

And this is the message which we have heard from him and announce unto you, that God is light, and in him is no darkness at all (1 John 1:5, ASV). *This is the message we have heard from him and declare to you: God is light; in him there is not darkness at all* (1 John 1:5, NIV).

John's readers receive from him exactly the same *"message"* (*epaggelia*) the Apostles received from Jesus. There is no better epistemology! The *"message"* relates to the moral nature of God, which is the proper beginning point in any discussion about sin.

God's Nature Stated Positively — *"God Is Light"*

The description *"God is light"* affirms His moral perfection. *"In him is no darkness at all"* declares His absolute ethical purity. Such an emphatic declaration about God's holiness is pivotal to John's subsequent discussion about sin and fellowship.

"Light" and *"darkness"* symbolize the contrasting extremes that separate good from evil. *"Light"* stands for 100% moral innocence. And *"darkness"* stands for sin or the perversions of morality. *"Light"* and *"darkness"* are natural enemies, hostile one to the other, and mutually exclusive. They do not co-exist, for the presence of one excludes the other. The same symbols are used to contrast *"love"* and *"hate"* (cf. 1 John 2:9-11). Paul used *"day"* and *"night"* as variations of John's symbols to illustrate the difference between *"knowledge"* and *"ignorance"* about the end of time (cf. 1 Thessalonians 5:4-8).

God's Nature Stated Negatively

The phrase *"no darkness at all"* insists that God is as hostile to sin as light is to darkness. God does not deal with moral relatives or ethical mixtures. No "gray" is allowed in those who have fellowship with Him. James affirms the uncompromising moral character of *"the Father of heavenly lights, who does not change like shifting shadows"* (James 1:17).

Clearly John establishes God's moral purity as the standard by which all ethical issues can be properly measured. Man needs standards that are both <u>perfect</u> and <u>external</u> to himself. He must not establish his own criterion of right and wrong. Paul says those who *"commend themselves"* by *"measuring themselves by themselves, and comparing themselves with themselves, are without understanding/are not wise"* (2 Corinthians 10:12, ASV). When man establishes his own standards and makes those standards the rule by which to live, he thereby standardizes whatever imperfections there are in his life.

John assures his readers that God has communion only with those who are morally sinless. He breaks fellowship with all to whom even one sin is imputed. That statement may appear to exclude everyone from fellowship with God, but it does not. John has already claimed apostolic *"fellowship with the Father and with the Son"* (1 John 1:3). He assures his readers that they too may have the same fellowship through *"the message we heard from him"* (1 John 1:5). Though John's statement does not exclude fellowship, it certainly does create the need for an explanation of the only basis on which it can exist — the blood of Jesus.

False Claims Concerning Fellowship With God

If we say [emphasis added] *that we have fellowship with him and walk in darkness, we lie, and do not the truth:"* (1 John 1:5, ASV). *If we claim to have fellowship with him yet walk in the darkness, we lie and do not live by the truth* (1 John 1:6).

Evidently John is exposing a distorted gnostic view about sin. He unmasks the *"lie"* of those who say that sin is not an obstacle to man's fellowship with God. Antinomian gnostics affirmed that sin is simply a physical act that does not impact the status of the soul. They claimed that the Spirit God is indifferent to fleshly sin. They denied that there is a God-given moral standard by which to live. Keeping commandments was foreign to their thinking (cf. 1 John 2:4). If their theology was right, they would have no need for any redemptive involvement by Jesus.

Gnostics would insist that Jesus liberated us from commandment keeping: *"It is for freedom that Christ has set us free . . . You, my brothers, were called to be free"* (Galatians 5:1, 13). Of course, they would be loathe to read the rest of those verses from Galatians. John rejects their theology on two counts. Their claim to fellowship is a *"lie."* And their *"walk"* is not according to *"the truth."* Fellowship is not determined by the "talk" but by the *"walk."*

The fellowship the Gnostics claimed is vertical because the *"we"* is anyone who presently *"walks in darkness"* and the *"him"* is God in whom *"there is no darkness at all."* It is important that the parties involved in this "talk" about fellowship be identified to help clarify who the *"one another"* of 1 John 1:7 is. For God to fellowship a man who *"walks in darkness"* would negate John's emphatic *"no darkness at all"* statement of 1 John 1:5.

Fellowship is defined by biblical synonyms that limit both human and divine involvements or communion. Fellowship implies working under the same yoke, joint participation, partnership, agreement, symphony, portion, concord, and mutual sharing in matters of common interest. Paul uses most of those synonyms in 2 Corinthians 6:14-16. God will not be *"yoked"* with wickedness; nor walk in *"harmony"* with sin. There is no *"communion between light and darkness"* and no *"concord between Christ and Belial."*

"If we say" is a catch phrase John uses again and again to expose and denounce unfounded assertions (cf. 1 John 1:.6, 8, 10; 2:4, 9; 4:20). Since the *"walk"* is a present active verb, it defines a settled practice of darkness which is John's portrait of sin. In Scripture a *"walk"* is a career, a life-style, or a profession. Note Paul's use of *"walk"* in Ephesians 2:2,10; 4:1,17; 5:8,15.

A *"walk"* has several characteristics. It has direction. It moves toward a destination. It has separation from its point of origin. A walk has progression. It is not static (it does not stand still). The Apostle Paul told Timothy, *". . . evil men and impostors will go from bad to worse, deceiving and being deceived"* (2 Timothy 3:13). A *"walk"* has companionships which are determined by the chosen direction it pursues, and therefore, the destiny toward which it progresses. A walk in darkness brings spiritual identity with Satan and his *"children"* (cf. 1 John 3:8-10). A walk in the light produces fellowship with God and His people. Thus a man who walks in darkness progressively moves deeper into darkness and toward eternal darkness (cf. Matthew 8:12; 25:30). There his companions in sin will be *"the devil and his angels"* (cf. Matthew 25:41). The lawless gnostics can not have fellowship with God in their settled practice of sin and the theological platform behind it.

The Possibility of Fellowship

But if we walk in the light, as he is in the light, we have fellowship one with another, and the blood of Jesus his son cleanseth us from all sin (1 John 1:7, ASV). *But if we walk in the light, as he is in the light, we have fellowship with one another, and the blood of Jesus, his Son, purifies us from all sin* (1 John 1:7, NIV).

There is a reversal of direction in the *"walk"* of 1 John 1:6 and 1:7. Fellowship between God and man does exist, but it is conditioned upon the essential character of God and man's consistent *"walk in the* (God's) *light."* This *"walk"* has the same attributes as the *"walk"* in 1 John 1:6. It is *"in the light,"* with increasing separation from *"darkness."* The *"walk"* of 1 John 1:7 qualifies the Christian to have *"the inheritance of the saints in the kingdom of light"* (Colossians 1:12). *"One with another"* (**met' allelon** = a reciprocating pronoun) is the fellowship already identified in 1 John 1:3. The *"one"* is a Christian and the *"another"* is God. The *"fellowship"* is between God and those who *"walk in the light,"* because that is the alleged claim to *"fellowship with God"* that John categorically denies in 1 John 1:6, but affirms in 1 John 1:7.

There are **three simultaneous actions** presented in 1 John 1:7. The **first** action is the **"walk."** It is a present active verb, subjunctive mood. The subjunctive *"if"* insists that the *"walk"* be *"in the light"* as a pre-condition to the other two concurrent actions. *"If"* that condition is of *"walking in the light"* is met, then we and God *"have fellowship one with another."*

The **second** action is **"have."** It is a present active indicative verb that defines the progressive and uninterrupted nature of our fellowship. The **third** action involves divine intervention when we sin while *"walking in the light."* It is the verb *"**cleanses**"* — a present active indicative verb. When we <u>keep on</u> *"walking in the light,"* we <u>keep on</u> having fellowship with the Father because the blood of Jesus <u>keeps on</u> *"purifying us from all sin."* To *"walk in the light"* is to walk under the blood of Jesus. That is the reason our sin does not break fellowship with God. Clearly *"walking in the light"* does not imply sinless perfection. If it did, there would be no need for the blood of Jesus to keep on cleansing us. The *"blood of Jesus . . . cleanseth us from **all** sin"* (1 John 1:7) at the baptistry (cf. Hebrews 9:14; 10:22; 1 Peter 3:21). This is the same *"blood"* that keeps post-baptismal sin from breaking the fellowship. His blood did not lose its cleansing power at the baptistry! Arising from the waters of baptism *"to live a new life"* (Romans 6:4), every Christian has a consciousness of purity. That same awareness of innocence should also accompany him as long as he *"walks in the light,"* because Jesus constantly stands as *"the propitiation/atoning sacrifice for our sins"* (1 John 2:2).

To *"walk in the light, as he is in the light"* does not define <u>our walk</u> as much as it defines <u>His light</u>. It says more about <u>where</u> we walk than about <u>how</u> we walk. By whose *"light,"* or by whose moral standards do we <u>walk</u>? If we measure each step by His moral perfection, make His *"light"* the rule of conduct, and hold His nature as the basis of all ethical decisions, then **we and He** have mutually rewarding companionship while the *"blood of Jesus"* keeps occasional sins from eroding the fellowship! Maybe an illustration or two would be helpful:

There are two men walking toward a common destiny. One of them stumbles and the other one lies down. Which one of the men gets up first? The stumbler does! He is embarrassed, but he gets up, dusts himself off, and continues his journey. But the other man, having lain down, has voluntarily given up both his walk and his planned destiny. The first man does not lose his fellowship with God, the second man does!

A man is given a fifty yard bolt of cloth, a pair of scissors, and a twelve inch ruler with instructions to cut the cloth into one foot pieces. Obviously, some of the cuts would be oblique here and there with occasional nicks in the cuts and off-line failures that are evident when the job is done. Not many of his pieces would be absolutely perfect, but every one of them would be cut according to the same perfect standard. So it is with our *"walk in the light"* as God reveals *"light."* **Our walk** is not always perfect, but **our standard** is consistently perfect. God credits us for our intent to measure each step according to His perfect *"light."*

John does not make any new claims. What he is teaching has been consistently taught by other inspired writers of his day. In Romans 8 Paul quoted David who said:

> *Blessed is he whose transgressions are forgiven, whose sins are covered. Blessed is the man whose sin the LORD does not count against him and in whose spirit is no deceit* (Psalm 32:1-2, NIV).

To *"count against"* (**ou'-me'logisetai**) is to make a legal entry of something in a log book. Even David knew about the blessedness of unrecorded sins. Paul said:

> *Therefore, there is no condemnation for those who are in Christ Jesus, because through Christ Jesus the law of the Spirit of life set me free from the law of sin and death. For what the law was powerless to do in that it was weakened by the sinful nature, God did by sending his own Son in the likeness of sinful man to be a sin offering. And so he condemned sin in sinful man, in order that the righteous requirements of the law might be fully met in us, who do not live according to the sinful nature but according to the Spirit* (Romans 8:1-4).

Our righteousness is not based on sinless performance but on the sinless perfection of Jesus

Some may be uncomfortable with John's affirmation that occasional sin does not break fellowship with God because that would appear to encourage the practice of sin. Paul faced the same misconception when Judaizers affirmed that his teachings about being *"justified by faith"* tended to undermine law-keeping and encouraged the practice of sin (cf. Romans 3:1-31). John says:

> *My dear children, I write this to you so that you will not sin. But if anybody does sin, we have one who speaks to the Father in our defense — Jesus Christ, the Righteous One* (1 John 2:1-2).

Someone might ask, "How many sins can a man commit and still be *"walking in the light"*? Such a question only confuses the issues under discussion. *"Walking in the light"* is not always determined by how many sins a person commits or does not commit. It defines whose *"light"* guides his *"walk."* He must walk in *"light"* as God's word reveals His truth as the standard. To *"walk in the light"* means the Christian strives to keep God's commandments (cf. 1 John 2:3) because Christians serve as the revelation of what God's *"light"* really is.

The phrase *"cleanses us from all sins"* assures the readers that the blood of Jesus covers every sin! When His *"blood cleanses ALL sins,"* how many sins remain? None, no not one! Can God fellowship those in whom there is no sin? Yes! In fact, they are the only persons He will fellowship!

The fact that the blood of Jesus keeps us clean is one of the highest motivations to clean living. When a Christian is spotlessly pure, wearing robes that have been *"made . . . white in the blood of the Lamb"* (Revelation 7:14), he naturally wants to stay clean! If he knows that he is already filthy in God's sight, what further damage can a little more filth do? Failure to appreciate the truths

John announces from Jesus tends to negate our gratitude for our spiritual innocence before God and compromises our motivation to holy living.

> *If we say that we have no sin, we deceive ourselves, and the truth is not in us* (1 John 1:8, ASV). *If we claim to be without sin, we deceive ourselves and the truth is not in us* (1 John 1:8).

A **second major gnostic error** is exposed here. The false claim of 1 John 1:6 results in the denial of any moral standard. In this verse some Gnostics seem to be saying, "There is a standard, and we are keeping it perfectly." Those making this claim are practicing Ascetics who have an exaggerated sense of their holiness and a degraded sense of God's truth. Through the practice of self-made rules of austerity, these men boast a spiritual elitism that is as vain as it is deceiving. This doctrine is rooted in the theory that the physical body is evil and that *"spirit"* people (as they like to call themselves) must live above the appetites of the flesh (cf. 1 John 4:1-6).

"If we say" is John's catch-phrase that identifies another error. The claim may well stem from a supposed, superior knowledge which the Gnostics believed endowed them with sin-resisting insights. Such vaunted, esoteric *gnosis*/knowledge gave them an enlightened status above those who were uninitiated into the mysteries. The Gnostics professed to be sinless just as the Pharisees who *"were confident of their own righteousness and looked down on everybody else"*(Luke 18:9). Their pretense of innocence easily identifies with ascetic impositions denounced by Paul. Their rules that said: *"Do not handle! Do not taste! Do not touch!"* (Colossians 2: 21) were based on human commands and teachings to create an external appearance of holiness. Paul said this kind of life-style of *"self-imposed worship, false humility, and their harsh treatment of the body"* lacked *"any value in restraining sensual indulgence"* (Colossians 2:23).

Through the Holy Spirit, Paul foresees on the near horizon further expressions of asceticism in the coming apostasy (*apostesontai*) when he said:

> *In later times some will abandon the faith and follow deceiving spirts and things taught by demons. Such teachings come through hypocritical liars, whose consciences have been seared as with a hot iron. They forbid people to marry and order them to abstain from certain foods, which God created to be received with thanksgiving by those who believe and who know the truth* (1 Timothy 4:1-3).

Monasticism became fully developed in several heretical groups during the first and second centuries.

Christians that are deceived is the tragic consequence of self-made standards of morality. The issue is then compounded by an unjustified assertion of perfect compliance. The Ascetics are neither sinless, thus the deception, nor do they have the proper standard — *"If we claim to be without sin, we deceive ourselves and the truth is not in us"* (1 John 1:8).

The ascetic gnostics of this verse are as much in need of the redemptive mission of Christ as are the antinomian gnostics of 1 John 1:6. The tragedy is that neither group acknowledged their need because of their doctrinal presuppositions. Their denial of sin introduces John's discussion on the confession of sins in 1 John 1:8-9.

> *If we confess our sins, he is faithful and righteous to forgive us our sins, and to cleanse us from all unrighteousness* (1 John 1:9, ASV). *If we confess our sins, he is faithful and just and will forgive our sins and purify us from all unrighteousness* (1 John 1:9, NIV).

There is a reversal of self-evaluation between 1 John 1:8 and 9. The Gnostic of verse 8 deceives himself by lying to himself about his sin. The honest believer of verse 9 stands accused before his own conscience (cf. 1 John 3:19) and before God's moral standard. He, therefore, admits to himself his sins.

"If we confess our sins" is a present subjunctive active verb that defines a settled practice when sins occur. This means there is a settled practice of confession rather than the fact that we are "generic" sinners. The promised forgiveness and cleansing are conditional upon the *"if"* that introduces the admission of sin.

"Confess" (***homologomen***) is a compound word that means to say the same word (***homo*** = same + ***logos*** = word). God already says the sin was committed. This verse requires that the sinner say the *"confess/same word"* that God has said. John does not say to whom the confession is made. It is easy to assume it is made to God. Since God foreknew our sins even before the cross, then this confession is not made for His information. We do not have to up-date God on our performance.

Obviously, the confession is the sinner's own acknowledgment to himself of wrong doing. Such an admission of need is the first step in any healing process. A patient admits to himself that he is ill before he visits the doctor. An alcoholic must first admit to himself his dependency before any recovery takes place. The publican of the parable *"went home justified before God"* (Luke 18:14) because he openly acknowledged his sins and his need for divine mercy. The Pharisee trusted in himself that he was righteous and prayed about himself. He assumed that God's judgment of him would be the same as his own judgment of himself. Being blind to his sin, he received no mercy. He did not ask for mercy because he denied the need (cf. Luke 18:9-14).

Notice Jesus' picture of the Pharisee: *"He stood and prayed thus* **with** *himself (****pros*** *= facing =* ***eauton*** *= himself)"* (Luke 18:11, ASV). Jesus indicates that the man either prayed *"to"* himself or was offering himself a prayer of self-congratulation before God. The NIV translates this as *"prayed **about** himself."* It is little wonder his unacknowledged sins were not forgiven.

The classic definition of sin is taken from an Old Testament statement about left-handed Benjamanite archers, *". . . every one could sling stones at a hair-breath, and not miss"* (Judges 20:16). *"Miss"* was translated in the Septuagint with the word ***hamartia***, which is the New Testament word for *"sin."* It literally means to miss the mark. Therefore, a confession of sin is an acknowledgment of some very fundamental facts:

1) It affirms that there **is** a "mark" — a moral standard that is set by God.
2) It admits deviation from the standard — "I have sinned."
3) It is an open declaration of need for God's mercy.
4) It would also have to issue a genuine expression of gratitude for standing forgiveness.

The man who is walking *"in the light, as he is in the light"* (1 John 1:7) is conscious of his sins and also aware of the cleansing blood of Jesus. He, therefore, lives a grateful but penitent life before God. He remembers that his sin does not reach the record book because he is under *"the blood of Jesus"* (1 John 1:7). Should he ask God to erase sin that has not been logged down against him? He does not deny his sin nor rationalize its commission. Clearly confession made to self is simultaneously made before God.

Some may oppose what John teaches in 1 John 1:7-9 and say that the *"confession"* is to God by saying that Jesus did teach us to pray, *"Forgive us our debts, as we also have forgiven our debtors"* (Matthew 6:12). But is this a prayer for forgiveness of debts from God, or is it not a request for a forgiving spirit toward our debtors? This could be a dangerous prayer because it asks God to be only as forgiving toward us as we are toward others. Matthew 6:14-15 explains both a blessing and a danger: *"For if you forgive men when they sin against you, your heavenly Father will also forgive you. But if you do not forgive men their sins, your Father will not forgive your sins."* The danger is that if we do not forgive men, then God will not forgive us.

John's *"If we confess our sins, he is faithful and just . . ."* (1 John 1:9) statement gives two elements of God's forgiving character — His fidelity and His righteousness. These are not simply abstract attributes of God's nature. They are divine qualities He manifests when He forgives us our sins and cleanses us from all unrighteousness. **First**, when John says *"He is faithful . . . and will forgive,"* his readers know that God promises forgiveness. As a promise-keeping God, He is reliable and trustworthy because He keeps Covenant with His people! **Second**, *"He is . . . **just/righteous** and will forgive"* because the cross at Calvary makes it right. Forgiveness does not demean God's moral standards nor compromise His personal righteousness. It declares that the cross has given Him the expediency that allows His lawful acquittal of sins. If a man trusts in Christ and His sacrifice with the biblical sense of the term *"faith,"* then it would not be *"right"* for God not to forgive the man's acknowledged sins. For that would result in double punishment: first of Christ and second the sinner, but both for the same set of sins.

Two additional statements are made about God's intervention on the sinner's behalf. **First**, *"He is faithful and righteous to **forgive** ('aphe) us our sins, . . ."* which means that forgiveness carries the concept of the dismissal of guilt just as if a debt is cancelled. **Second**, God **cleanses** *"us from all unrighteousness."* The cleansing insists that the stain of sin is removed much as a leper was *"cured"* of his disease (cf. Matthew 8:2). *"All sins"* (1 John 1:7) and *"all unrighteousness"* (1 John 1:9) assures the Christian that he does not live under the jeopardy of his sins. He lives as a saint and not as a sinner.

> *If we say that we have not sinned, we make him a liar, and his word is no in us* (1 John 1:10, ASV). *If we claim we have not sinned, we make him out to be a liar and his word has not place in our lives* (1 John 1:10, NIV).

John uses the phrase *"If we say"* this time to expose the **third** and most grievous claim of the gnostic followers because it makes God Himself the liar! If the question of guilt for sin comes down to a debate between God and man, then *"let God be true, and every man a liar"* (Romans 3:4). Just to make sure that none be deceived in merit, Paul affirms that God's law speaks to men who are under the law, *"Now we know that whatever the law says, it says to those who are under the law, so that every mouth may be silenced and the whole world held accountable to God"* (Romans 3:19). God is already on record! He said, *"All have sinned* (aorist tense which means it is man's past record) *and fall short* (present indicative tense which is talking about man's present condition) *of God's glory"* (Romans 3:23, ASV).

In 1 John 1:10 the phrase *"we have not sinned"* is a perfect tense verb, which means it is the boast of a gnostic perfectionist. He claims a history of moral purity that also characterizes his present life. He may either be the radical ascetic (cf. 1 John 1:8) or the antinomian (cf. 1 John 1:6) who denies the reality of sin. In either case his theology makes God a liar because God says that *"all have sinned"* (Romans 3:23). There is evident ignorance of the fact that *"God cannot lie"* (Hebrews 6:18) and that His Word is absolute truth (cf. Ephesians 1:13; Colossians 1:5-6). The real liars do not have God's Word in them. God is a witness to every sin ever committed by every man! What forgiveness can be expected from God if a man accuses Him of being a *"liar"?*

It will be helpful to remember that John's argument continues to flow into the early verses of the next chapter.

APPLICATION

Fellowship with God in the life to come is conditional upon fellowship in the here and now. The fellowship between God and man as the most sacred of relationships must be guarded with unparalleled spiritual tenacity. The greatest enemy of our union with God is Satan and his greatest tool to disrupt that union is our sin. Therefore, a tender conscience that has been educated about sin from the Word of God is the greatest protector of our daily walk with God. The provisions God made at the cross assure us that our sin is no surprise to him. Therefore, it is vitally important that open, objective, and honest confession of sins and repentance before God be kept as a daily expression of our trust in His mercy. That is the only avenue to the confident assurance that John discusses throughout this epistle.

The First Epistle of John

Fellowship is Rooted in the Forensic Advocacy of Jesus

1 John 2:1-2

My little children, these things write I unto you that ye may not sin. And if any man sin, we have an advocate with the father, Jesus Christ the righteous (1 John 2:1, ASV). *My dear children, I write this to you so that you will not sin. But if anybody does sin, we have one who speaks to the Father in our defense — Jesus Christ the Righteous One* (1 John 2:1, NIV).

In chapter 1 John affirmed that the blood of Jesus keeps a Christian's sins from being recorded in God's "log book." Lest some assume that such constant cleansing is an encouragement to sin, John writes to dismantle that assumption. In fact, he says, *"I write this so that (hina = in order that) you will not sin."* Divine forgiveness is not a license to sin. Do the kisses, robe, shoes, fatted calf, and the forgiveness of the Father in Luke 15: 11-27 encourage the prodigal son to return to the pig-pen? Does God's grace encourage sin? Paul's violent disclaimer to this question was, *"God forbid!"* (Romans 6:2, ASV). Sin in the face of the high price of *"propitiation"* (1 John 2:2, ASV) discredits the cross, cheapens divine grace, and exposes the sinner's ignorance of heaven's sacrifice for forgiveness!

The phrase *"so that you will not sin"* insists that John's purpose is to promote holy living among his *"little children."* He encourages their personal sanctification. Peter argues, *"He himself bore our sins in his body on the tree,* **so that** *we might* **die to sins** *and* **live to righteousness***; by his wounds you have been healed"* (1 Peter 2:24). John's phrase, *"if any man sin"* assumes the fact that they will sin.

"We have an advocate/one who speaks" is court-room language — sin is a legal matter as well as a moral issue. Sin is a violation of law. John says, *"in fact, sin is lawlessness"* (1 John 3:4). *"Advocate"* (**parakleton**: **para** = along side + **kaleo** = call) is a term applied by the Greeks to the one who acted as the counsel for the defense. Literally, it means the one who is called to one's side to plead his cause when he stands accused before the judge.

The phrase *"with the Father/to the Father"* identifies the place where Jesus defends the guilty. It is at the bar of Divine justice! When the accused call upon Jesus to defend them against the penalties due their wrong doing, He readily intervenes. His advocacy is a vital part of His ongoing ministry for the saints. Jesus *"always lives to intercede for them"* (Hebrews 7:25) and presently appears *"for us in God's presence"* (Hebrews 9:24). It is His intervention that keeps the believer's sins wiped clean from God's record book. Herein is John's explanation of how God's acquittal of the guilty does not compromise His righteousness. If only we could understand how God manages our sin through Jesus, maybe it would be easier for us to understand how we can handle our standing before Him.

"Jesus Christ the righteous" is our lawyer. We must be impressed with God's apparently favorable inclination toward the guilty who call upon Jesus as their defense. Here is the scene! *"The Father"* is the judge in all sin matters; *"Jesus Christ"* is the court-appointed lawyer for the defense. He is the Son of the Judge, and *"with Him I* (God) *am well pleased"* (Matthew.3:17; 17:5). Jesus is a sympathetic brother to the accused –

> *For we do not have a high priest who is unable to sympathize with our weaknesses, but we have one who has been tempted in every way, just as we are — yet was without sin* (Hebrews 4:15).

Jesus Christ is *"the Righteous One."* Not only does He qualify to serve as our trusted *"Advocate,"* He also is effective before God when He intervenes on our behalf. It is said that Perry Mason, the legendary lawyer of TV fame, never lost a case. The reason is simple. He always defended the innocent ones. Jesus, our heavenly Lawyer, has never lost a case either when His accused brethren call upon His advocacy. And yet He always defends those who are guilty!

What plea should a sinner make before this court? He must know that both the Judge and the Advocate were there when he sinned. As witnesses of the sin, they have the evidence. The Judge is *"righteous to forgive"* (1 John 1:9) only on predetermined conditions; the Advocate is righteous to defend on the same basis (cf. 1 John 2:1-2). To deny the sin (as the Gnostics of 1 John 1:8, 10) is to deceive the guilty, make the Judge a *"liar,"* and preclude for himself any chance for acquittal. The honest course of action is to plead guilty as accused and then call for the *"Advocate/"Righteous One"* to defend him.

This is an unusual court because a guilty plea receives a verdict of acquittal. Such a forensic release of the accused is powerfully acclaimed by Paul when he says, *"Who will bring any charge against those whom God has chosen? It is God who justifies"* (Romans 8:33).

> *And he is the propitiation for our sins; and not for ours only, but also for the whole world* (1 John 2:2, ASV) *He is the atoning sacrifice for our sins, and not only for ours but also for the sins of the whole world* (1 John 2:2, NIV).

The phrase *"he is* [Emphasis added] *the propitiation"* means that He satisfies God's justice — He is *"the atoning sacrifice for our sins."* Our sins were judicially punished in Jesus when *"He himself bore our sins in his body on the tree, so that we might die to sins and live to righteousness; by his wounds you have been healed"* (1 Peter 2:24). **"Is"** (*estin*), as a present indicative verb of being, defines Jesus' <u>standing role</u> as the One who has already paid all our sin-debts before God. If He had not, then some further atonement would have to be made. The word *"propitiation"* explains why the guilty one goes free when Jesus is his *"Advocate."* Jesus does not deny the guilt of his brother who sinned. He simply pleads for acquittal based on the fact that He personally paid the penalty that was due — *". . . He was taken away . . . For he was cut off from the land of the living; for the transgression of my people he was stricken"* (Isaiah 53:8).

"Propitiation" (**hilasmos**) is a significant redemptive term that is rich in both Old and New Testament usage. It conveys in both Testaments the concept of divine appeasement or satisfaction for offended justice and violated law. God's wrath against the sin has been judicially placated by the cross (cf. Romans 3:24-26).

Our sense of justice is offended when some unscrupulous lawyer abuses our judicial system to obtain a verdict of innocence for those who are really guilty. Such action frustrates the court; it makes a sham of the law. Justice is frustrated because the crime goes unpunished. No such injustice is done when God forgives those whom Christ defends for *"he is the propitiation."* The sin has already been tried, judged, and sentenced. Its penalty has already been executed by the **vicarious** (experienced through another person, Ed.) death of Jesus because God made, *"him who had no sin to be sin for us, so that in him we might become the righteousness of God"* (2 Corinthians 5:21).

John says, *"Not for our sins only, but also for the whole world"* which affirms that Jesus' sacrifice was not just for an elite few as some Gnostics might claim. This verse also dismantles the Calvinistic view of limited atonement — that Jesus died only for those predestined to eternal salvation. John wants all his readers to acknowledge the universal validity of the cross as God's atoning sacrifice (cf. 1 John 4:14). The church's universal mission assignment grows out of many such New Testament declarations (cf. Matthew.28:18-20; Mark 16:15; 2 Corinthians 5:14-21; 1 Timothy 2:3-5).

Jews instantly understand John's *"propitiation"* terminology.

In the Mosaic sacrificial system the word was closely tied in with the lid covering the *"mercy-seat"* in the Hebrew tabernacle. That is where sacrificial blood was sprinkled on Yom Kippur (the Day of Atonement) making it possible for Israel's sins to be symbolically placed on the head of *"the goat for Azazel"* and then to be removed from the camp (cf. Leviticus 16:12-22). *"Atonement"* is involved in the idea of *"propitiation,"* because it implies that the sin is covered — that is the root meaning of **"kippur,"** the Hebrew word for *"atonement"* in the Old Testament. Prophetically the Father foresaw *"the suffering of his* (Jesus') *soul* (in the crucifixion), *he will see the light of life and be satisfied; by his knowledge my righteous will justify many, and he will bear their iniquities"* (Isaiah 53:11). *"Be satisfied"* is *"propitiation."* Look for other New Testament texts that use *"propitiation"* and examine the vicarious sacrifice of Jesus in each one (cf. Romans 3:25; Hebrews 2:17; 1 John 4:10). It was God who graciously initiated the process of appeasement through the atoning sacrifice of Jesus Christ.

Fellowship Is Rooted in Obedience to God's Commands

1 John 2:3-6

And hereby we know that we know him, if we keep his commandments (1 John 2:3, ASV). *We know that we have come to know him if we obey his commands* (1 John 2:3, NIV).

The phrase *"we know that we have come to know him"* presents two *"knows"* that have different verb tenses. The first *"know"* is present indicative, and it defines the present perception and practical grasp of the believer's knowledge about God. The second *"know him"* is a present perfect verb. It insists that they have come to know God and that knowledge still stands. *"Hereby"* is the first of **nine times** that John gives the criterion by

which **true knowledge of God** can be tested. It is no surprise that
the **first test** is **commandment keeping.**

The phrase *"we know him"* includes the believer's knowledge
of God's moral nature, His legislation of ethical standards, and His
innate hostility to sin. All of these the Gnostic denies or ignores.

The phrase *"if we keep"* is a present subjunctive that makes
keeping commandments an ongoing obligation for those who
know God. *"Keep his commandments"* can be defined as
"walking in the light." The real proof of fellowship is evident
when we *"walk as Jesus did"* (1 John 2:6). It is essential that one
"know" God's commandments because they are the revelation of
His ethical nature. To know God is to know His commandments.
But knowing God is theoretical, while keeping His
commandments is both functionally practical and fellowship
assuring.

> *He that saith, I know him, and keepeth not his*
> *commandments, is a liar and the truth is not in him* (1
> John 2:4, ASV). *The man who says, 'I know him,' but*
> *does not do what he commands is a liar, and the truth is*
> *not in him* (1 John 2:4, NIV).

The phrase *"He that saith I know him"* exposes an empty
antinomian claim. The boast here is as much a lie as that of 1 John
1:6 when they claim to have fellowship with God. Clearly the
Gnostic does not believe in moral standards nor feel obliged to
keep commandments. In chapter 1 the fellowship issue is settled
by the way they *"walk"* and not their talk. Here the issue of real
knowledge of God is determined by an obedient work not a hollow
word. The god Gnostics claim to *"know"* is not concerned with sin
or laws. John's epilogue, *"My little children, guard yourselves*
from idols" (1 John 5:21, ASV) seems to imply that the Gnostic's
god is a man-made idol. That god does not exist! He certainly is
not the *"God"* that John knows.

The phrase *"the truth is not in him"* is characteristic Hebrew
redundancy. John makes a positive statement, and then

emphatically reinforces it with a negative thought of equal significance. This man neither has a real god nor lives by moral guidelines.

> But whoso keepeth his word, in him **verily** hath the love of God been perfected. Hereby we know that we are in him (1 John 2:5, ASV) [Emphasis added]. But if anyone obeys his word, God's love is **truly** made complete in him. This is how we know we are in him (1 John 2:5, NIV) [Emphasis added].

The word *"keepeth/obeys"* is a present subjunctive verb that defines a settled obedience to God's commandments. In fact, the Christian keeps on keeping God's Word. Christians know that law keeping is neither redemptive nor the root of redemption. Redemption is the **fruit** of law-keeping.

The word *"verily/truly"* (**alethos**) stands in stark contrast with the *"lie"* (**pseustes**) of the pseudo-intellectual Gnostic in 1 John 2:4. Paul says, *"Turn away from godless chatter and the opposing ideas of what is falsely called knowledge"* (1 Timothy 6:20). It is vain to call Jesus, *"Lord, Lord,"* and not to do the things He says to do (cf. Luke 6:46).

The phrase *"the love of God/God's love"* is objective genitive that has God as the object — hence our love for Him. Our love for Him *"is truly made complete/perfected"* when God's Word is kept through our obedience to Him. Obedience is the response of love and the spring-board of fellowship with God. Jesus said, *"If anyone loves me, he will obey my teaching. My Father will love him, and we will come to him and make our home with him"* (John 14:23). The *"perfected"* does not speak of absolute proof of a believer's affection, it simply implies that obedience achieves the end that love for God demands. John has further insights on love that has been made complete in 1 John 4.

> He that saith he abideth in him ought himself also to walk even as he walked (1 John 2:6, ASV). Whoever

claims to live in him must walk as Jesus did (1 John 2:6, NIV).

The phrase *"He that saith/Whoever claims"* insists that the believer's claim to union with God be confirmed by practical and demonstrated obedience. To *"abide (**menein**) in him"* is to reside with him. Such intimate fellowship imposes a strict life-style.

The word *"ought/must"* (**opheilei**) conveys more sober commitments than may be implied by our modern usage of the word. It imposes a sense of moral indebtedness that **must be paid**. Paul's discussion on the mutual ministry of husbands and wives illustrates the impact the word *"ought"* carries. He told the Corinthians, *"Let the husband render to the wife her **due"** (**opheilomenon** = debt) *and likewise the wife unto the husband"* (1 Corinthians 7:3). Failure to pay what is due (what is owed) constitutes violence to the matrimonial privilege. The New International Version says:

> *The husband should fulfill his marital duty to his wife, and likewise the wife to her husband. The wife's body does not belong to her alone but also to her husband. In the same way, the husband's body does not belong to him alone but also to his wife. Do not deprive each other . . . (1 Corinthians 7:3-5).*

The American Standard Version says, *"Defraud ye not one to the other . . ."* Fraud is the failure to pay a debt. John properly insists that the privilege of fellowship with God creates a moral indebtedness to obey His commands.

The phrase *"walk even as he walked"* establishes Jesus as the model of love **for** and obedience **to** God. Jesus said, *"If you obey my commands, you will remain in my love, just as I have obeyed my Father's commands and remain in his love"* (John 15:10; cf. John 14:31). *"As he walked"* perfectly summarizes the whole life of Jesus. Particularly relevant to commandment keeping is the new commandment issued by Jesus in John 13:34. Paul's imperative injunction, *"Live a life of love, just as Christ loved us . . .* (Ephesians 5:2) concurs with John's stated obligation to *"walk as he walked."*

Fellowship Is Rooted In Keeping
The New Commandment

1 John 2:7-11

Beloved, no new commandment write I unto you, but an old commandment which ye had from the beginning: the old commandment is the word which ye heard (1 John 2:7, ASV). *Dear friends, I am not writing you a new command but an old one, which you have had since the beginning. This old command is the message you have heard* (1 John 2:7, NIV).

John uses the literary form of a paradox to emphasize his point. He gives *"no new commandment . . . but an old one."* Then one verse later (1 John 2:8), he shows the reality of the *"new commandment."* Possibly John wants his readers to understand that he is not issuing new rules about love, but is simply reiterating the *"old/new commandment"* Jesus gave some fifty years earlier.

The phrase *"from the beginning"* does not relate to the beginning of Genesis 1:1 nor to the *"love your neighbor as yourself"* assignment given to Israel in Leviticus 19:18. A *"new command"* implies that there was also an *"old"* one. The "Golden Rule" is based on the love standards of the Law of Moses. The old standard demanded equal devotion to others as to self; it insisted on reciprocity of treatment (cf. Matthew 5:38; Leviticus 24:20). Jesus applied His *". . . do to others what you would have them do to you . . . "* to the old Levitical rule. That is the indication of His statement, *". . . for this sums up the Law and the Prophets"* (Matthew 7:12). If John 13:34 only restates previous laws on love, then Jesus did not really give a *"new command"* at all. The commandment *". . . which you had since the beginning"* must refer either to the beginning of Christ's new love assignment in John 13:34 or to the believers' introduction to the love commandment at the time of their conversion.

The word *"new"* (**kainon**) in Greek conveys the concept of something new in <u>time</u> and new in <u>kind</u>. It is the same *"new"* as Jeremiah's promise of a *"new covenant"* (cf. Jeremiah 31:31-34; Hebrews 8:8). Clearly John does restate Jesus' commandment, because he says, *"This old command is the message you <u>have</u> <u>heard.</u>"* What they had *"heard"* would be the instructions from the Apostles to Christians which said, imitate the love Jesus had commanded and made noble by His sacrifice.

> *Again, a new commandment write I unto you, which thing is true in him and in you; because the darkness is passing away, and the true light already shineth* (1 John 2:8, ASV). *Yet I am writing you a new command; its truth is seen in him and you, because the darkness is passing and the true light is already shining* (1 John 2:8, NIV).

What is *"new"* about the *"new commandment?"* It is not simply love because that was enjoined in the Levitical legislation. It is a *"new"* standard of love, based on a *"new"* intensity of devotion to the needs of others. It is the **". . .As I have loved you, . . . "** from John 13:34. It is the **"new"** element of love for **new covenant** people. Jesus loved beyond self, completely sacrificing Himself for others' needs. With unreserved surrender of life, He gave all that deity can give when He *"emptied himself,"* and then He gave all that humanity can give when He *". . . humbled himself . . . even unto. . . the death of the cross"* (Philippians 2:7-8). This is a **new** standard of love that was unknown until Calvary. In fact, John says, *"This is how we know what love (agape) is: Jesus Christ laid down his life for us. And we ought to lay down our lives for our brothers"* (1 John 3:16). The example of Jesus becomes the *"new,"* one hundred percent perfect, standard of love for

Christians to imitate. Just as there is a perfect moral standard (cf. 1 John 1:5), there is also a perfect *"love"* standard.

This new standard of *"love — is true in him."* *"True"* stands for reality — John is talking about the real/true nature of love. Jesus not only gave the new command; He was really the practical and perfect concrete expression of love. This new standard of love is also *"true in you"* — the believers who learned to imitate Jesus in sacrificial love. Those early Christians so loved that they *"had everything in common"* (Acts 2:44); and *"no one claimed that any of his possessions was his own, but they shared everything they had"*(Acts 4:32). Some of them endured great suffering and were exposed to public insults and persecution (cf. Hebrews 10:32-33). Some of them would lay down their lives for Christ (cf. John 16:2). What Jesus promised became reality — *"By this all men will know that your are my disciples, if you love one another"* (John 13:35).

The phrase *"the darkness is passing away and the true light already shineth"* is the result of what happens when the *"new"* commandment is practiced. *"Light"* and *"darkness,"* as antithetical elements, seem to symbolize here the light of love and the darkness of hate. With the spread of Christ's love as a standard, the night of human hatred gives way to a new day of love in society. Clearly Christ ushered in a new world order. The Hebrew writer uses the phrase *"the world to come"* (Hebrews 2:5; cf. Hebrews 6:5; 9:11; 10:1). Love for others is the new world's platform for success and the badge of identity of its citizens.

The genuine *"light"* is *"the true (**alethinon**) light."* in contrast to the counterfeit claim in 1 John 2:9. The adjectival suffix *"inos"* denotes the substance of which things are made, therefore, it stands in opposition to superficial imitations of love or empty words that are unconfirmed by appropriate actions of service.

> He that saith he is in the light and hateth his brother, is in the darkness even until now (1 John 2:9, ASV). Anyone who claims to be in the light but hates his brother is still in the darkness (1 John 2:9, NIV).

The claim to be *"in the light"* is absolutely negated by *"hate"* for a brother because *"light"* and *"darkness"* do not co-exist. The gnostic elitist despises any disciple of Jesus who rejects his philosophical presuppositions. Their intellectual snobbery led them to condemn others in the same way the Pharisees did when they said, *". . . this mob that knows nothing of the law — there is a curse on them"* (John 7:49). They *"were confident of their own righteousness and looked down on everybody else"* (Luke 18:9). John attributes that same Pharisaical separatism and intolerance to the Gnostics. Their claims to esoteric, cosmic knowledge gave them an exaggerated sense of self importance and consequent hostility toward those who remained faithful to apostolic teaching.

The phrase *"in darkness even until now"* clearly affirms that Gnostics never escaped the spiritual darkness of their background. The new birth cannot arise from a platform of hate because *"everyone who loves has been born of God and knows God"* (1 John 4:7). John settles the issue when he says, *"They went out from us, but they did not really belong to us . . . their going showed that none of them belonged to us"* (1 John 2:19). John confirms this position again: *"We know that we have passed from death to life, because we love our brothers. Anyone who does not love remains in death"* (1 John 3:14). To **love not** is to **live not.!**

He that **loveth** his brother **abideth** in the light, and there is no occasion of stumbling in him" (1 John 2:10, ASV) [Emphasis added]. *"Whoever loves his brother lives in the light, and there is nothing in him to make him stumble* (1 John 2:10, NIV).

The words *"loveth"* and *"abideth"* are present indicative verbs in a compound sentence which makes them complementary. Present love confirms present residence in light. Whatever is required to receive the new birth is exactly what is required to keep it, and vice-versa.

The phrase *"no occasion of stumbling (skandalon) in him"* has two possible applications. The first could affirm that the one who loves does not himself stumble in his walk. 1 John 2:11 would lend credence to this first view. Jesus said: *"If a man walk in the day, he stumbleth not, for he seeth the light of this world. But if a man walk in the night, he stumbleth, because the light is not in him"* (John 11:9-10; cf. Psalms 119:165).

The second possible application would affirm that the one who loves does not cause others to stumble in their walk. In either case, love for the brethren is a powerful deterrent to sin among Christians.

> *But he that hateth his brother is in the darkness, and walketh in the darkness, and knoweth not whither he goeth, because the darkness hath blinded his eyes* (1 John 2:11, ASV). *But whoever hates his brother is in darkness and walks around in the darkness; he does not know where he is going, because the darkness has blinded him* (1 John 2:11, NIV).

Intense light can *"blind."* But John says it is the *"darkness"* of hate that blinds men. The man who hates does not see; he is blinded by his hate. Paul said, *"The god of this age has blinded the minds of unbelievers, so that they cannot see the light of the gospel of the glory of Christ, who is the image of God"* (2 Corinthians 4:4). The *"god of this world"* is at work among men.

Note the on-going process at work here. *"Hates"* is a present participle which means this man keeps on hating. *"He is in darkness"* is a present indicative which defines his current standing. *"Walks around in darkness"* is also a present indicative that exposes his persistent practice. *"Does not know"* is a present perfect which indicates past ignorance that continues into the present. *"Blinded"* is an aorist active which means there has been an indefinite past surrender to hatred! This verse defines exactly what the ravages of hate bring to the hater!

The phrase *"knows not whither he goeth"* indicates naivete about the dire consequences of hate. In contrast with 1 John 2:10, the one who hates *"stumbles"* himself and causes others to fall in sin.

Fellowship Is Rooted In True Knowledge About God And Satan

1 John 2:12-14

I write unto you, my little children, because your sins are forgiven you for his name's sake (1 John 2:12, ASV). *I write to you, dear children, because your sins have been forgiven on account of his name* (1 John 2:12, NIV).

The word *"write"* is a present indicative referring to this epistle. The *"little children"* in verse 12 are joined to the *"fathers"* and *"young men"* in 1 John 2:13. John does not seem to deal with chronological ages of the three groups but with their spiritual age in Christ. The *"little children"* would be recent converts and would be the most vulnerable when exposed to gnostic errors and doubts about their fellowship with God. Gnostics aggressively denied that those who accepted apostolic testimony were true Christians (cf. 1 John 2:26). What better assurance could John give them than the knowledge that their *"sins are forgiven."* *"Are forgiven"* is a present perfect tense verb. The perfect tense defines past completed, action that has a point of beginning. The present part of the verb structure defines the present, linear (continuing) result of that past action. Here John affirms **"standing"** forgiveness as a present possession based on their past obedience to Christ. Even immature Christians do not live under the menace of their sins.

The phrase *"for his name's sake"* is the ground upon which sins *"are forgiven."* The *"name"* first represents Jesus and then His atoning sacrifice. Baptism *"in the name of Jesus Christ"* (Acts 2:38) is by His authority, and it results in *"the forgiveness of sins"* (Acts 2:38). Peter emphatically states, *"'It is by the name of Jesus*

Christ of Nazareth, . . . Salvation is found in no one else, for there is no other name under heaven given to me by which we must be saved'" (Acts 4:10, 12).

> *I write unto you, fathers, because ye know him who is from the beginning. I write unto you, young men, because ye have overcome the evil one* (1 John 2:13a, ASV). *I write to you, fathers, because you have known him who is from the beginning. I write to you, young men, because you have overcome the evil one* (1 John 2:13a, NIV).

The words *"I write"* refers again to this present epistle. *"Fathers"* could be John's definition of mature Christians whose stability in Christ removes any concern for their faith. *"You know him"* refers to their knowledge through personal experience growing out of fellowship with Him. John says they *"know"* His moral perfection, His commandments, His love assignment, and their obligation to walk even as He walked.

The *"young men"* obviously have resisted gnostic efforts to sway their convictions and their practice. The *"evil one"* is a direct reference to the Devil who is behind the perversions of Gnosticism. John gives pointed warnings about Satan's work (cf. 1 John 3:8, 10; 4:4; 5:18). The word *"overcome"* is a present perfect verb indicating that they have won a **lasting** battle over error just as the *"children"* in 1 John 2:12 have gained **lasting** forgiveness of sins.

> *I have written unto you, little children, because ye know the father* (1 John 2:13b, ASV). *I write to you, dear children, because you have known the Father* (1 John 2:13b, NIV).

1 John 2:13 should have terminated with John's present message to the three groups: *"children, fathers and young men."* And 1 John 2:14 should have begun at *"I have written unto you, little children"* because John's verb tenses change from the present indicative of *"I am writing"* (1 John 2:13a) to an aorist of *"I have*

written" (1 John 2:13b) which defines some former correspondence from John.

The phrase *"I have written"* could point either to John's Gospel or to the Revelation letter. What John formerly had to say (and here repeats) to the *"little children, fathers and young men"* seems to correlate better with the message from Revelation than with the gospel of John. John's Gospel was written *"that you may believe that Jesus is the Christ, the Son of God, and that by believing you may have life in his name"* (John 20:31). Revelation was written to assure Christians of their ultimate victory over all opposition.

John says, *"You know the Father"* to show that even the recent converts to Christ had embraced the apostolic declaration that *"God is light"* (1 John 1:5) and His commandments must be kept. They stand united with the older disciples who also *"know the Father."*

> *I have written unto you, fathers, because ye know him who is from the beginning. I have written to you, young men, because ye are strong, and the word of God abideth in you, and ye have overcome the evil one* (1 John 2: 14, ASV). *I write to you, fathers, because you have known him who is from the beginning. I write to you, young men, because you are strong, and the word of God lives in you, and you have overcome the evil one* (1 John 2:14).

The *"fathers"* were secure in their settled knowledge of God when John had written to them earlier. Even now their perception of Him remains unchanged. *"Him who is from the beginning"* is referring to Christ, but the phrase may recall *"the beginning of their confidence"* in Him at conversion as in Hebrews 3:14.

John applauds their success story by saying, *"You have over come the evil one."* There are **two reasons for their success** in overcoming Satan. The **second** reason: *"the word of God abides in you"* is the basis for the **first** reason: *"you are strong."* *"The* *word of God abides in you"* acknowledges their acceptance of God's commandments as the standard of their walk. Their power to resist the intrusion of error and temptation to sin is based on the sound moral theology and doctrinal revelations of the apostolic message. The Christian's power to resist Satan comes from a well cultivated understanding of, and practical obedience to, the truth of God's Word. (cf. John 8:32-34; Ephesians 6:10ff.).

Fellowship Is Rooted In The Christian's Love For God

1 John 2:15-17

Love not the world, neither the things that are in the world. If any man love the world, the love of the father is not in him (1 John 2:15, ASV). *Do not love the world or anything in the world, the love of the Father is not in him* (1 John 2:15, NIV).

In this extended context, the word *"world"* is used six times to signal its opposition to spiritual values. It is the *"world"* that is manipulated by the lusts that drive its ambitions. *"Love not"* is an imperative injunction against the surrender of the affections to anything that could become an obstacle to spiritual maturity in *"overcoming the evil one"* (1 John 2:13, 14).

The word *"love"* (**agape**), as defined in the *"new commandment,"* is sacrificial devotion to a worthy object. But neither the *"world"* John discusses here nor its *"things"* are appropriate subjects of this self-surrendering affection. John condemns any *"love"* that stands in opposition to our *"love for the Father."* The Christian must conquer and overcome all illicit attractions the world offers.

The words *"the world"* could stand for *"life in this world"* which Jesus taught His disciples to *"hate"* (John 12:25) when survival in the world would result in the loss of fellowship with God. Demas abandoned his mission with Paul because *"he loved this world"* (2 Timothy 4:10). Perhaps, he felt that his association with one who said, *"I die daily"* (1 Corinthians 15:31) could get them both killed. Demas was too attached to this world to lose his life here, so that he could *"keep it for eternal life"* (John 12:25).

*"The **things** that are in the world"* are as much a menace to a Christian as is the *"world"* itself. These *"things"* can be the world's value systems, its cultural "mores," its perverted ideals, its hedonistic pursuits, and its secular humanism as they are organized under the dominion of Satan. To *"love the things of the world"* would involve participation in the world's life-style, and therefore, cause one to share in its destiny.

"The love of the Father is not in him" because it is impossible to give simultaneously sacrificial devotion to two opposing entities. James said, *". . . friendship with the world is hatred toward God"* (James 4:4). Jesus Himself said, *" 'No one can serve two masters'"* (Matthew 6:24). There are two *"worlds"* with which a Christian must deal. Jesus *"gave himself for our sins, that he might deliver us out of this present **evil world"*** (Galatians 1:4, ASV). There is another "new world order" of the Messianic kingdom. The Messiah's world extends into God's world beyond time. That is the only "world" that is worthy of all sacrificial surrender. Paul instructed the Colossians, *"Set your hearts on things above, . . . set your minds on things above, not on earthly things"* as his imperative command to the redeemed (Colossians 3:1-2).

> For all that is in the world, the lust of the flesh and the lust of the eyes and the vainglory of life, is not of the father, but is of the world (1 John 2:16, ASV). For everything in the world — the cravings of sinful man, the lust of his eyes and the boasting of what he has and does — comes not from the Father but from the world (1 John 2:16, NIV).

John defines the extensive attraction the world contributes to the reign of veil with *"All that is in the world."* The *"god of this world"* (2 Corinthians 4:4, ASV) uses man's physical and emotional needs to entice him into moral compromise. There is much debate, even among the most reputable commentators, concerning the extent of John's *"all."* Does he imply that this triad of lusts embraces and exhausts **all** the avenues of sin? Or does he simply make a generic statement about *"all that is in the world"* as **all** that the world has to offer and then proceeds to give three examples among the many available options?

It would appear that John's *"all"* covers **all** possible sins. At least the two most classical episodes of temptation easily fall within John's three-in-one language: Adam and Eve (cf. Genesis 3:6) and Jesus (cf. Matthew 4:3-9). It is difficult to imagine a sin — any sin — that does not fit into at least one of the three categories of lust presented here. In any case, it is clear that this world can gratify only the animal appetites of man and offers nothing to feed his soul. Jesus taught that a man's life is more than food, drink, and clothing (cf. Matthew 6:25-34).

Sometimes *"lust"* (**epithumia**) in Scripture is illusive in its import. It can be good as in Luke 22:15 (ASV), *"With desire (**epithumia**) I have desired (**epithumesa**)"* or it can be evil as in Galatians 5:17 (ASV), *"The flesh lusteth (**epithumei**) against the spirit."* Lust is defined as a strong, even overflowing, desire. Desires are constitutional, innate, and therefore, essential for existence. There are no God-given needs that cannot be satisfied lawfully. And yet, all such appetites can become a target of perverted gratification in sin. James 1:14-15 explains how Satan uses man's *"desire"* first to *"draw him away"* from moral standards, and then *"entices him to sin."* Only then does lust become vicious because it ends in death.

The *"lust of the flesh"* springs from internal, physical appetites for things one does not have. Why would a man lust for what he already possessed? This *"lust"* could be for the very things Jesus promised God would supply his people: food, drink, and clothing (cf. Matthew 6:25-34). When physical needs are sought outside God's providence, then trust in God is replaced by unlawful ways of procurement. For Eve, the fruit of the forbidden tree was evidently *"good for food"* (Genesis 3:6). For Christ, the appeal was to *"turn stones to bread"* (Matthew 4:3). In both cases, the *"lust of the flesh"* was the avenue of temptation.

The *"lust of the eyes"* are those external attractions or things which a person does not possess. The sight of unlawful pleasures excites a man with the anticipation of sensual fulfillment. Covetousness, envy, and greed feed on visual or imagined objects of delight. Even a blind man could be victimized by *"lust of the eyes."* Clearly the desire for illicit relations fits this category (cf. Matthew.5:28). For Eve the forbidden fruit *"was pleasing to the eyes"* (Genesis 3:3). For Jesus the temptation arose from the vision of *"all the kingdoms of the world and their splendor"* (Matthew 4:8). The *"eyes"* became the source of enticement for each.

The phrase *"the vainglory (alazoneia) of life"* is the boastful pride and ostentatious display of things a man does possess. Such empty show of abilities or properties ignores that all we are and have come from God. High-minded vanity of this sort causes one to *"be arrogant and . . . put their hope in wealth, which is so uncertain"* and not *"to put their hope in God, who richly provides us with everything for our enjoyment"* (1 Timothy 6:17). This *"vainglory"* could cause a woman to dress immodestly with *"braided hair, or gold or pearls or expensive clothing"* (1 Timothy 2:9). A man could be tempted the same way by being prideful over his physique, his heritage, or his holdings. For Eve, the appeal came from what Satan said, *"You will not surely die . . . your eyes will be opened, and you will be like God, knowing good and evil"* (Genesis 3:4-5). For Jesus, Satan appealed to His ability to miraculously jump off the highest point of the temple and thus dazzle the people with the spectacle of divine intervention (cf. Matthew 4:5-6).

Man fell into sin by the prohibited feeding of his appetites, by the unholy gratification of his imaginations, and by seeking undeserved dignities. Man's salvation from the fall is through Jesus who reversed the process. Pride on the part of Adam and Eve brought all mankind down, humility (the opposite of pride) on the part of Jesus restores all believers to Eden's fellowship with God.

The phrase *"is not of the Father"* denies any secret understanding between God and man's temptation to sin (cf. James 1:12-13). Paul said:

No temptation has seized you except what is common to man. And God is faithful; he will not let you be tempted beyond what you can bear. But when you are tempted, he will also provide a way out so that you can stand up under it (1 Corinthians 10:13).

The phrase *"comes not from the Father but from the world"* traces all unholy deeds to the world's magnetic pull away from *"the light"* of God's revealed standard. This *"world"* that *"hates you"* (1 John 3:13) is the world that speaks worldly philosophies and *"the world listens to them"* (1 John 4:5). This is the *"world"* that John speaks of when he said, *"the whole world is under the control of the evil one"* (1 John 5:19). And yet it is also the same world that Jesus spoke of when he said, *"For God so loved the world that he gave his one and only Son"* (John 3:16) — God sent His Son to be the Savior of the **"world"** (cf. 1 John 4:14).

And the world passeth away, and the lusts thereof: but he that doeth the will of God abideth forever (1 John 4: 17, ASV). *The world and its desires pass away, but the man who does the will of God lives forever* (1 John 2:17, NIV).

The phrase *"the world and its desires pass away"* becomes a strong motive for resisting the allurements of the world. Both the *"world"* and the *"desires of the world"* will not endure. God's children, on the other hand, will live forever. It is folly to trade the eternal for the transient.

The phrase *"passeth away"* literally means **is** passing away. The heart should not be set on that which is already in the process of decay. The *"world"* and its *"darkness/paragetai"* are passing away (cf. 1 John 2:8) — both are in a state of disintegration. John's rationale for the imperative command not to love this *"world"* nor its *"lusts"* is inspired and extremely practical. Love for any of this impedes proper love for the Father. *"The world and* *its desires"* can gratify only the sensual appetites of man. They are Satan's tools to destroy fellowship with God. They are temporary in duration while God's values are eternal.

Fellowship Is Rooted In Apostolic Epistemology

1 John 2:18-29

> *Little children, it is the last hour: and as ye heard that antichrist cometh, even now have there arisen many antichrists; whereby we know that it is the last hour* (1 John 2:18, ASV). *Dear children, this is the last hour; and as you have heard that the antichrist is coming, even now many antichrist have come. This is how we know that it is the last hour* (1 John 2:18, NIV).

When John refers to *"the last hour,"* it is really *"a last hour,"* since there is no definite article. Though the *"last hour"* is **eschatological** (having to do with the doctrine of the "last things," Ed.) terminology, it does not signal the end of time. It is an omen of dramatic change on the horizon. Clearly the *"last hour"* (**eskate hora**) is already present in John's time as the arrival of *"many antichrists"* provides the confirmation.

In his gospel, John often uses the *"hour"* to indicate decisive moments in the history of redemption (cf. John 2:4; 4:21-23; 5:25-28; 7:30; 8:20; 12:23; 16:2, 4, 25, 32; 17:1). The tragic appearance of *"many antichrists"* with their immoralities and anti-Christian theologies will introduce traumatic change in the religious scene and atmosphere surrounding the church.

The phrase *"as you have heard"* stirs memories of the warnings from John or other inspired writers about the eminent apostasy. Jesus spoke of them as wolves *"in sheep's clothing"* (Matthew 7:15). Paul spoke of *"the man of lawlessness"* and *"the man doomed to destruction"* (2 Thessalonians 2:3). Peter used the terms *"false prophets"* and *"false teachers"* (2 Peter 2:1). John

called them *"antichrists"* and *"deceivers"* (2 John 7).
Jude said:

> *For certain men whose condemnation was written about long ago have secretly slipped in among you. They are godless men, who change the grace of our God into a license for immorality and deny Jesus Christ our only Sovereign and Lord* (Jude 4).

The phrase *"many antichrists have come"* indicates the diverse moral and theological mixture they brought with them. Gnosticism was not monogenetic (having developed from one single thing or thought, Ed.) or uniform in theology. *"Even now"* many different schools of gnostic thought *"have arisen"* to menace the church in John's day. *"Antichrist"* was a present reality and not some future "Armageddon" opponent yet to appear in connection with a supposed millennial reign on earth. Their presence among the true believers confirms John's *"last hour"* situation.

The prefix *"anti"* stands for an adversary of everything Christ represents to the Christian. It is not simply a "pseudo christ" or false claimant to the office of Messiah (cf. Matthew.24:24; Mark 13:22). John considers the Gnostics denial of the humanity of Jesus to be the over-arching spirit of the movement (cf. 1 John 4:3). They also strongly deny the deity and messiahship of Christ. They affirm that the purpose of His mission was not to save man from sin but from the prison of the body. It is no wonder John calls them *"antichrist."*   John gives numerous characteristic marks whereby his *"little children"* could easily identify *"antichrist."* They were divisive and sectarian; they never accepted apostolic testimony about Christ and were not Christians (cf. 1 John 2:19). They were *"liars"* who denied that Jesus is the Messiah and rejected the "Father/Son" relationship (cf. 1 John 2:22). They were militantly seeking proselytes for their cause (cf. 1 John 2:26). As false prophets, they denied that Jesus Christ came in the flesh; their theologies arose from secular sources; and they were driven by the spirit of error (cf.1 John 4:1-6). As *"deceivers and the antichrist,"* their doctrines menace the believer's *"full reward"* (cf. 2 John 7-8). Anyone who supports their cause *"shares in his* (their) *wicked work"* (2 John 9-11). Obviously, Diotrephes was one on the *"antichrist"* (cf. 3 John 9).

> *They went out from us, but they were not of us; for if they had been of us, they would have continued with us: but they went out, that they might be made manifest that they all are not of us* (1 John 2:19, ASV). *They went out from us, but they did not really belong to us. For if they had belonged to us, they would have remained with us; but their going showed that none of them belonged to us* (1 John 2:19, NIV).

In this verse John uses the preposition *"of"* (***ek***) three times and the pronoun *"us"* (***hemon***) five times. He has a "they/you" and a "them/us" emphasis in 1 John 2:19-27 to unmask *"them"* and to reaffirm *"us."* Their voluntary departure from the church should not distress *"us,"* because *"none of them belonged to us."* They associated for a while with the church, and perhaps were even ritually baptized upon a confession of faith in a **docetic** Jesus — one that only seemed to be human. If their conversion had been genuine, that would mean they had accepted apostolic testimony about Jesus and *"they would have remained with us."* Their separation probably resulted in the formation of other churches or denominational assemblies; and that gave John the confirmation that *"none of them belonged to us."*

John had already affirmed that they are *"in darkness even until now"* (1 John 2:9, ASV). Whatever claim they may have made about having fellowship with God (based on their supposed personal sinlessness and deep knowledge of God) is a compound lie.

> *And ye have an **anointing** from the holy one, and ye know all things"* (1 John 2:20, ASV) [Emphasis added].

*But you have an **anointing** from the Holy One, and all of
you know the truth* (1 John 2:20, NIV).

Having exposed the Gnostics, John here returns to address the
"little children/dear children" of 1 John 2:18. *"You"* is a second
person plural pronoun that embraces all genuine Christians — *"all
of you know the truth."* There is nothing in Christianity that is just
for the elite as the Gnostics often claimed. John is presenting the
Christian's **epistemology** (their source of knowledge) that was
originally from Jesus to the Apostles, then from the Apostles to all
believers. The apostolic message is *"the message we have heard
from him* (Jesus) *and declare to you"* (1 John 1:5). All Christians
possess the complete revelation that came from *"the Holy One,"*
who patently is Jesus. The *"Holy One"* in Messianic prophecy and
New Testament fulfillment is Jesus (cf. Psalms 16:10; 89:18;
Isaiah 12:6; 49:6; Acts 13:47; Mark 1:24; Luke 4:34; John 6:69;
Acts 3:14). Gnostics rejected the Apostles and have a different
source of alleged knowledge (cf. 1 John 4:5).
    The phrase *"you have an anointing (**krisma**)"* is an external
possession, just as *"we have an Advocate"* in 1 John 2:1. John
does not say that his *"little children"* had been "anointed" as the
Gnostics boasted about themselves. The *"anointing"* is defined by
what the *"anointing"* does! John gives ample information by
which the identity of the *"anointing"* is established, but before that
data is discussed, it will be helpful to document some gnostic
claims.
    In a document cited by Hippolytus (an early post-apostolic
writer) as representing a gnostic sect known as the Naasenes, he
says: "We alone of all men are Christians, who complete the
mystery at the third portal and are anointed there with a speechless
chrism." There is a reference made to this in the Ante-Nicene
Fathers (Vol. 5 page 58) and Philosophuma (Volume 9, page 121-
122). It is also evident that those Gnostics practiced elaborate
anointing rituals to initiate their adherents into the mysteries of
knowledge. With such an introduction into *"knowledge/**gnosis**,"*
then they assumed that their speculative theologies were
undeniable reality. Paul said:

See to it that no one takes you **captive** *through hollow and deceptive philosophy, which depends on human tradition and the basic principles of this world rather than on Christ* (Colossians 2:8) [Emphasis added]. John says, *They are from the world and therefore speak from the viewpoint of the world, and the world listens to them* (1 John 4:5).

Evidently John uses the gnostic claim of being "anointed" and even employs that ceremonial terminology to inform believers that in reality it is the believers who have the only valid *"anointing."* He assures Christians that they have an *"anointing"* in the message Jesus gave them through apostolic witness and testimony about the truth.

What insights does John give about the *"anointing"* and what is accomplished through it? The *"anointing"* is the source of all knowledge; all Christians have it because it came through Christ Jesus (cf. 1 John 2:20). It is the *"truth"* that has already been taught to believers. It is authentic (cf. 1 John 2:.21). It exposes the lie of *"antichrist"* and affirms that Gnostics are not Christians (cf. 1 John 2:19, 22-23). The *"anointing"* is *"what you have heard from the beginning"* (1 John 2:24); it is the apostolic message that *"remains in you"* (1 John 2:27), the believers; and it is that message which gives fellowship with *"the Father and his Son, Jesus Christ"* (1 John 1:3; cf. 1 John 2:24). It brings the promise of *"eternal life"* (1 John 2:25). It contains vital warnings against *"those who are trying to lead you astray"* (1 John 2:26). The *"anointing"* was received from Christ *"from the beginning"* and remains in them; it excludes the need for other teachers because *"his anointing teaches you about all things"* (1 John 2:27). Since *"that anointing is real, not counterfeit"* (1 John 2:27), its message is trustworthy. The *"anointing"* insists that Christians stay with their convictions and *"remain in him"* (1 John 2:27). The emphasis of the entire context about the *"anointing"* is on the **message** and not the messenger. There will be more discussion about the *"anointing"* in the verse by verse exegesis.

I have not written unto you because ye know not the truth, but because ye know it, and because no lie is of the truth (1 John 2:21, ASV). *I do not write to you because you do not know the truth, but because you do know it and because no lie comes from the truth* (1 John 2:21, NIV).

The phrase *"you do know"* excludes any further revelations and eliminates the need for other teachers. If they already *"know the truth,"* why does John write it to them again? This answer is of critical importance both to John and other New Testament writers. They write to **reconfirm truths** already taught, to expose the *"lie"* and counter the "liar" who teaches it, and to give permanent form and record of the truth. Peter's reasons for writing are clearly stated:

> *So I will always **remind** you of these things, even though you know them and are firmly established in the truth you now have. I think it is right to **refresh your memory** as long as I live in the tent of this body, because I know that I will soon put it aside, as our Lord Jesus Christ has made clear to me. And I will make every effort to see that after my departure you **will always be able to remember** these things* (2 Peter 1:12-15) [Emphasis added].

Peter wanted Christians to remember the truths they had been taught, to *"stir* them *up"* (ASV) by reminding them of the importance of the truth, and to give them a permanent record of the message he had received that would last beyond his life-span. They needed to know that after he was gone there would be no other valid source of information about the cause of Christ. Paul frequently reminded the brethren of truths taught, believed, embraced, and treasured because it is by those truths that Christians are saved (cf. 1 Cor.15:1-2; 1 Cor.10:23; 2 Thessalonians 2:5).

*Who is **the** [Emphasis added] liar but he that denieth that*

Jesus is the Christ? This is the antichrist, even he that denieth the Father and the Son (1 John 2:22, ASV). *Who is the liar? It is the man who denies that Jesus is the Christ. Such a man is the antichrist — he denies the Father and the Son* (1 John 2:22, NIV).

The words *"the liar,"* (with **the** definite article) seem to affirm that such a denial of Jesus as Messiah is the supreme lie! B. F. Westcott says that anyone who denies that Jesus is the Messiah is guilty of the "master-falsehood." A. E. Brooke says such a man is "the liar par excellence, in whom falsehood finds its complete expression." John may be targeting Cerinthian Gnosticism which claims that Jesus was an *aeon*, meaning that He originated as deity that descended upon and invaded Jesus' body at the time of His baptism and departed from Him before His crucifixion. The *"liar"* John deals with rejects the messianic role of Jesus (the fact that He is the Christ) and even rejects the Father's testimony about His Son (cf. 1 John 5:9-10).

Whosoever denieth the Son, the same hath not the Father: he that confesseth the Son hath the Father also (1 John 2:23, ASV). *No one who denies the Son has the Father; whoever acknowledges the Son has the Father also* (1 John 2:23, NIV).

Someone who *"has the Father"* enjoys spiritual union with Him in the church family. Anyone who *"denies the Son"* does not have this fellowship and is as godless as the Gentiles without Christ (cf. Ephesians 2:11-12). Since *"the Son"* is the only means of access to the Father (cf. John 14:6; Acts 4:12), it is crucial that He be confessed (cf. Romans 10:9-10). Confession of Jesus on earth is prerequisite to being confessed by Jesus before the Father in heaven (cf. Matthew 10:32). Without acknowledging the **Sonship** of Jesus there is no salvation.

John says, *"If anyone acknowledges that Jesus is the Son of God, God lives in him and he in God"* (1 John 4:15). That person has been given the Holy Spirit to confirm his family ties with the

Father and the Son (cf. Ephesians 1:13-14; 1 John 3:24; 4:13).

> *As for you, let that abide in you which ye heard from the beginning.* **If** [Emphasis added] *that which ye heard from the beginning abide in you, ye also shall abide in the Son, and in the Father* (1 John 2:24, ASV). *See that what you have heard from the beginning remains in you.* **If** [Emphasis added] *it does, you also will remain in the Son and in the Father* (1 John 2:24, NIV).

John begins this paragraph with *"As for you"* (ASV) as an emphatic contrast to the *"liars"* he spoke about earlier. *"See that what you have heard from the beginning* **remains** *in you"* is a permissive imperative that **intensifies** the urgency of consistent reliance upon the original apostolic message. J. W. Roberts indicates that John doubles up the personal pronouns for emphasis: *"As for* **you,** *let what* **you** *heard . . . abide in* **you, you** *also shall abide."* Evidently John holds them responsible for what they knew was the apostolic message. *"If"* is a conditional particle which makes loyalty to the truth that was *"heard from the beginning"* prerequisite to spiritual union with the Father and the Son. John reconfirms the issues at stake in 2 John 9: *"Anyone who runs ahead and does not continue in the teaching of Christ does not have God; whoever continues in the teaching has both the Father and the Son."* John states the positive and the negative of continuing in the teachings of Christ and the doctrines about Him.

The phrase *"abide in the Son/remain in the Son"* precedes *"in the Father,"* because the Son is the only avenue to fellowship with the Father. *"And this is the promise which he promised us, even the life eternal"* (1 John 2:25, ASV). *"And this is what he promised us — even eternal life"* (1 John 2:25, NIV).

The phrase *"the promise which he promised us"* restates John's **theme subject** of **life with the Father** (cf. 1 John 1:2). Eternal life is a **present** possession (cf. 1 John 5:13). *"Eternal"* describes the quality of the life. This life solidly rests on the conditional *"abiding in the Son"* from 1 John 2:24.

The same word for *"promise"* (**epaggelia**) is frequently used in the New Testament for a message or an announcement (cf. I John 1:2, *epaggelia*). Since John is dealing with God who is righteous, the very fact that He announces certain blessings upon His people automatically makes the announcement a sure *"promise"* (cf. 2 Corinthians1:20).

> *These things have I written unto you concerning them that would lead you astray* (1 John 2:26, ASV). *I am writing these things to you about those who are trying to lead you astray* (1 John 2:26, NIV).

John returns to his discussion of *"them"* to issue words of warning about the intent of these false teachers. They were militantly aggressive in their efforts to proselyte Christians to their philosophies. In 2 John 8 he imperatively demands that the church *"Look to yourselves, that you lose not the things which we* (the Apostles) *have wrought, but that you receive a full reward"* (ASV). Souls are in jeopardy whenever Christians listen to false teachers. The present participle *"trying"* says that Gnostics are unsuccessfully *"trying to lead you astray."*

The word *"astray"* (*planonton*) is the same word used for the men who are self deceived (*planomen*) by claiming sinless performance (cf. 1 John 1:8). John considers his words of wisdom sufficient warning.

> *And as for you, the anointing which ye received of him abideth in you, and ye need not that anyone teach you; but as his anointing teacheth you concerning all things, and is true, and is no lie, and even as it taught you, ye abide in him* (1 John 2:27, ASV). *As for you, the anointing you received from him remains in you, and you do not need anyone to teach you. But as his anointing teaches you about all things and as that anointing is real, not counterfeit — just as it has taught you, remain in him* (1 John 2:27).

The best defense against *"those who are trying to lead you astray"* is the *"anointing you received from him* (Jesus)*"* As long as what they heard from the beginning from the Apostles remains in them, then they do not need any gnostic teachers. The apostolic message acts as their teacher concerning all things. The Lord's testimony is true and does not lie. The only reliable teacher for the Christian is *"his anointing"* — Jesus is its only source.

A Christian's epistemology is rooted in apostolic epistemology. The Apostles' knowledge came by sense perceptions (sight, sound, feel, contemplation) during their three year association with Christ and from His revelation to them in the message they heard from Him (cf. 1 John 1:1-5). The Apostles are the believer's only avenue to the divine message. Both Luke and the Hebrew writer trace their epistemology to the Apostles, who in turn traced theirs to Jesus (cf. Luke 1:1-4; Hebrews 2:1-4).

A corroborating parallel to this verse is found in 1 John 5:20: *"And we know also that the **Son of God** has come, and has given us understanding, so that we may know him who is true. And we are in him who is true — even in his Son Jesus Christ."* The **"holy one"** of 1 John 2:20-21 is the **"Son of God"** in this verse. In 1 John 2:20-21 Jesus gave *"the anointing"* and in 1 John 5:20 He gives *"understanding."* In both contexts the content is true and real. It is not counterfeit nor is it a lie.

So what is the **"anointing"**? Evidently, it is the all sufficient **Word of God** which John, the Apostle, had heard directly from Jesus, then *"declared"* it verbally to his *"little children,"* and then proceeded to write it down to reconfirm its truthfulness and authenticity (cf. 1 John 2:21). The Apostles *"are from God and whoever knows God listens to us, but whoever is not from God does not listen to us"* (1 John 4:6). Those who hear the message of the Apostles will hear the same message they got from Jesus. This is the way Christians come to **"know"** God.

Another confirming parallel passage is found 2 Tim.3:14-16. Paul wants Timothy to stay with his epistemological source:

> *But abide thou in the things which thou has learned and has been assured of, knowing of whom thou hast learned them; . . . the sacred writings which are able to make*

thee wise unto salvation through faith which is in Christ Jesus. Every scripture inspired of God is also profitable for teaching, for reproof, for correction, for instruction which is in righteousness: that the man of God may be complete, furnished completely unto every good work (ASV).

And now, my little children, abide in him: that, if he shall be manifested, we may have boldness, and not be ashamed before him at his coming (1 John 2:28, ASV). *And now, dear children, continue in him, so that when he appears we may be confident and unashamed before him at his coming* (1 John 2:28, NIV).

John adds his imperative injunction that Christians must remain in Jesus (*"him"*) just as the *"anointing"* teaches them to do. The practical conclusion to John's exhortation is to *"abide in him — remain in him — continue in him."*

The phrase *"if he shall be manifested"* (*phanerothei*) is a definite reference to the second coming of Jesus at some indefinite time. In view of that certain event, *"abiding in him"* becomes even more imperative. Redemption from past sins through Christ's first coming is vitally significant in view of His second coming.

The phrase *"abide in him"* is followed by a *"so that"* (*hina*) clause, and it relates to having *"boldness (parresian) . . . before him at his coming (parousia)."* John will mention again the Christian's encounter with Jesus when He comes again (cf. 1 John 3:2; 4:17).

"Boldness" is the Christian's freedom of speech. It suggests a child's confident dialogue with a loving father rather than the shameful fear of a slave. The child of God feels confident, cheerful assurance in his relation with his heavenly Father. Assurance of present fellowship with God gives the Christian confidence that *"if he shall be manifested, we shall be like him; for we shall see him even as he is"* (1 John 3:2).

John uses the phrase *"and not be ashamed before him"* to describe the awful position the lying, deceiving antichrist will have when Christ comes — his *"fear hath punishment"* (1 John 4:18).

Imagine the consternation and dismay of those who have denied His humanity, His deity, and His messiahship at the revelation of the *"Lord Jesus . . . from heaven in blazing fire with his powerful angels"* (2 Thessalonians 1:7).

> *If ye know that he is righteous, ye know that everyone also that doeth righteousness is begotten of him* (1 John 2:29, ASV). *If you know that he is righteous, you know that everyone who does what is right has been born of him* (1 John 2:29, NIV).

The phrase *"if ye know (**eidete** — from **oida**)"* is the strong settled knowledge of the moral nature of the coming Christ. The phrase *"God is light"* (I John 1:5) not only defines His moral excellence, it is an assignment for those who desire fellowship with Him. It certainly leads them to *"walk as Jesus walked"* (1 John 2:6).

The words *"doeth righteousness"* form a present participle defining a settled, habitual practice of righteousness. John identifies the empirical evidence of the new birth — it is in holy living!

The words *"is begotten"* are perfect passive indicative that confirms how Christians are the passive beneficiaries of God's regenerative activity in the new birth. The new birth can occur only when *"everyone . . . believes that Jesus is the Christ . . . born of God"* (1 John 5:1). The new birth also demands a determined commitment to righteous living as this verse affirms.

The First Epistle of John

Fellowship Is Rooted In Our Status As Children

1 John 3:1-3

Behold what manner of love the Father hath bestowed upon us, that we should be called children of God; and such we are. For this cause the world knoweth us not, because it knew him not (1 John 3:1, ASV). *How great is the love the Father has lavished on us, that we should be called the children of God! And that is what we are! The reason the world does not know us is that it did not know him* (1 John 3:1, NIV).

The reference in 1 John 2:29 about being *"begotten of God"* easily suggests the *"children of God"* relationship in 1 John 3:1. The word *"Behold"* (***Idete*** = aorist imperative) can encourage visual inspection (as it is used in John 6:36) or, as in this verse, it commands that the object be seen with the mind, an encouragement to think about something.

John uses the language of surprise in his *"What manner (**potapen**) of love"* statement — ***potapen*** suggests amazement, even admiration. It is an un-earthly love; it belongs to another world. In fact, the literal meaning of the word ***potapen*** when it is translated *"what manner"* is really *"of what world."*

This same word is used in other contexts. Notice the impact of the word: *"What manner of man...even the winds and the sea obey him"* (Matthew 8:27) and Mary's surprising exclamation of *"What manner of salutation"* (Luke 1:29) that is evoked from her by the angelic annunciation (cf. Mark 13:1; 2 Peter 3:11). It is the

Father's love that is the object of John's wonderment. He presents several reasons that motivate his imperative command to *"behold"* or to contemplate God's love for his children:

1) Consider the object of God's love: *"us"!* This is the same *"us"* of Romans 5:6-11 which says we are *"weak, ungodly, sinning enemies."* at just the right time

2) Look at the *"bestowed"* (**dedoken**) nature of God's love. It was neither deserved nor earned by us — it is a gift!

3) Do not ignore the amazing **status** God's love grants. We are called *"children of God."*

4) This is not simply a lofty title, it is a concrete reality. John says, *"and such we are."*

5) Great admiration is expressed over our ultimate, common identity with Christ in spiritual essence. That will be verified when we see Him and we *"shall be like him, for we shall see him as he is"* (1 John 3:2).

6) Maybe it is not amazing that *"the world does not know us* because *"it did not know him."* The *"knows us not"* implies that *"the world"* does not acknowledge our family tie with God simply because Gnostics make that claim about themselves. For them, our rejection of their presuppositions excludes the possibility of our fellowship with God.

Beloved, now are we children of God, and it is not yet made manifest what we shall be. We know that, if he shall be manifested, we shall be like him; for we shall see him even as he is (1 John 3:2, ASV). *Dear friends, now we are children of Gd, and what we will be has not yet been made known. But we know that when he appears, we shall be like him, for we shall see him as he is* (1 John 3:2, NIV).

Our present status as *"children of God"* has definite bearing on our future conformity of nature with Christ when *"he shall be manifested.*" The Apostle Paul generally used the term *"sons of God"* (*huios*) to identify the Christian's adoption into the family. John prefers the term *"children"* (*tekna*) for it stresses the birth process of entry into God's household.

It is evident that gnostic dogma, relative to the alleged intrinsic evil of the physical body, conditioned their thinking about the disposition of the body when Jesus comes. Like the Sadducees who denied the resurrection, Gnostics would resist the concept of the *"redemption of the body"* (Romans 8:23). In fact, they held that the primary mission of Jesus' second coming was not to save the body from the grave (cf. Hebrews 9:28), but rather to save the soul from the body. It is easy to imagine arrogant gnostic questions about the functions of a physical body in the spirit world of the resurrection. They could see the body as an obstacle in their visionary world of eschatology. That is no problem for John's concept of the eternal kingdom of Christ.

The phrase *"not yet made manifest"* assures us that our future glory has not been made a matter of divine revelation. No event in the ministry of Jesus on earth clearly shows anything about the future condition of God's people. *"What we shall be"* beyond this life has not *"yet been made manifest,"* neither in the transfiguration of Jesus nor in His resurrection appearances.

One thing John said *"we know"* for certain, and *"we know"* it by revelation, is that **"we shall be like him."** Clearly, what we now are, Jesus once was; what He now is, we one day will be. The proof that *"we shall be like him"* centers in the revelation that *"we shall see him as he is."* If He were to appear in His present glorified human body, with the eyes of our present *"body of humiliation"* we would not be able to see Him. But when He *"fashions anew the body of our humiliation, that it may be conformed to the body of his glory"* (Philippians 3:21, ASV), then we will be able *"to see him even as he is."* Using Paul's definitions about our present body, it is *"corruptible, dishonorable, weak, natural, earthly and mortal"* (cf. 1 Corinthians 15:42-54). But in the resurrection, our body will be made *"incorruptible, glorious, powerful, spiritual, heavenly and immortal"* (cf. 1 Corinthians

15:42-54). With such eyes, *"we shall see him even as he is"* (cf. Matthew 5:8; 1 Corinthians 13:12). "face to face"

> *And every one that hath this hope set on him purifieth himself, even as he is pure* (1 John 3:3, ASV). *Everyone who has this hope in him purifies himself, just as he is pure* (1 John 3:3, NIV).

The words *"this hope"* define the Christian's aspiration of seeing Jesus and of becoming like Him when He comes. This *"hope"* is *"set on him"* (**ep' auto**) — literally our hope is resting upon Jesus. The fact of our constant *"cleansing by the blood of Jesus"* (1 John 1.7, 9), and of our future when He *"will transform our lowly bodies so that they will be like his glorious body"* (Philippians 3:21) does not encourage sinful living; instead it encourages the Christian to live a pure life. The Christian finds a higher motivation to personal purity of life and life-style in such divine grace. To *"do righteousness"* (1 John 2:29) discloses the ethical obligations our salvation imposes upon us.

Motivated by the expectation of *"being like Jesus,"* the hopeful Christian *"purifies himself, just as he is pure."* The Christian cannot personally *"purify"* himself of his sin, but he can certainly cease **the practice** of it. The disciple knows that it is Jesus who *"cleanses us of all unrighteousness"* (1 John 1:9).

The phrase *"even as **he** is pure"* establishes the standard of Jesus' ethical purity as the Christian's model in life. True disciples desire to be sinless as a reasonable response to redemption. They actively strive for personal holiness in life. It is not an absurd or unreasonable quest. Resisting temptation requires the denial of lusts and the suppression of fleshly desires, for *"he who has suffered in his body is done with sin"* (1 Peter 4:1).

The word *"purifies"* (**agnizei**) is distinguished from *"holy"* (**agios**) by the fact that **agios** is initial purity. **"Agnizei"** is purity that is gained and sustained through holy zeal and personal piety in life. This verse demands sincere consecration that results in the cleansing of the heart and the hand (cf. James 4:8).

APPLICATION

These concepts about God's love are eternal and therefore as valid today as for John's generation. The assurance that Christians will see God beyond this life stimulates their confident expectation and maintains their expectation of heaven. That hope constantly challenges us to purge sin from our lives as a noble aspiration for believers today to *"walk as he walked."*

Fellowship Is Rooted
In A Settled Practice Of Righteousness

1 John 3:4 - 10

Every one that doeth sin doeth also lawlessness: and sin is lawlessness (1 John 3:4, ASV). *Everyone who sins breaks the law; in fact, sin is lawlessness* (1 John 3:4, NIV).

The phrase *"everyone who sins"* is a present active participle which sets those who go on practicing sin against those who actively seek to eliminate sin from their lives (cf. 1 John 3:3). Sin is not simply a mistake, a social indiscretion, a mere shortcoming, or an error of judgment! Sin is much more critical.

John says, *"Sin is lawlessness!"* This is John's definition of its nature and its character. Sin is the stubborn refusal to be governed by moral norms. *"Lawlessness"* comes from the compound Greek word ***anomia*** (***a*** = anti + ***nomos*** = law + ***ia*** = practice). The practicing sinner is either wanton in his disdain for ethical standards, or else he defiantly holds a theology that rejects the existence of moral rules. Without a doubt John is posed to refute antinomian gnostic thinking in their claim that sin is irrelevant both to God and man.

And ye know that he was manifested to take away sins:

and in him is no sin (1 John 3:5, ASV). *But you know that he appeared so that he might take away our sins. And in him is no sin* (1 John 3:5, NIV).

If sin makes no difference in a man's relationship with God, then why did Jesus *"appear so that he might take away our sins"*? *"Take away"* (*aire*) means that He lifted up and carried away the sin (cf. Mark 6:29; John 2:16). He came to *"save his people from their sins,"* (Matthew 1:18) not *"in"* their sins. His mission is clearly defined as God's remedy from the devastating consequences sin brings to mankind.

John defines Jesus' perfect innocence and His moral perfection with *"in him is no sin."* His vicarious sacrifice demanded that He be *"blameless"* (cf. Hebrews 7:26; 9:14). The Hebrew writer said, *"It is impossible for the blood of bulls and goats to take away sin"* (Hebrews 10:4), *"so Christ was sacrificed once to take away the sins of many people"* (Hebrews 9:28; cf. 1 John 3:8).

Whosoever abideth in him sinneth not; whosoever sinneth hath not seen him, neither knoweth him (1 John 3:6). *No one who lives in him keeps on sinning. No one who continues to sin has either seen him or known him* (1 John 3:6).

The word *"lawlessness"* produces a settled practice of sin because God's laws do not restrain "lawless" people. When John says, *"live in him,"* he uses a linear present participle that denotes a standing fellowship with God while *"walking in the light"* (1 John 1:7). This kind of relationship with God can never exist where there is a present practice of sin. John's *"walking in darkness"* discussion in chapter 1 negates the possibility of such a person *"living in him."*

"Whosoever sinneth," is a present participle which defines a career of sin — it means there is the settled practice of a moral renegade then or now. Such a man has not seen God and does not

know Him. The perfect tense of both *"seen"* and *"known"* indicates past blindness and ignorance about God's moral nature that persists as a standing result into the present. John has already affirmed that only those who *"practice righteousness"* can be *"born of God"* (1 John 2:29). That excludes anyone who *"walks in darkness"* (1 John 1:6), does not keep God's commandments, *"hates his brother"* (1 John 2:9,11), and anyone who is lawless from fellowship with God (cf. 1 John 2:4).

Obviously this man has never become a Christian for he has never *"seen"* or *"known"* God. There is no contradiction between what John affirms here and what he taught in 1 John 1:8 and 10. In those verses, he was dealing with a monastic perfectionist who makes up his own standards or else he had in mind a committed antinomian who denies the existence of any legislated standard of conduct. The child of God does sin occasionally (cf. 1 John 1:7, 9), but sin is the exception rather than the rule of his life.

Since John uses the present tense of habitual practice, he is insisting that those who *"live/abide in him"* do not maintain a consistent lifestyle of sin. Christians do not continually live in violation of the moral standards revealed in God's commandments.

My little children, let no man lead you astray: he that doeth righteousness is righteous, even as he is righteous (1 John 3:7, ASV). *Dear children, do not let anyone lead you astray. He who does what is right is righteous, just as he is righteous* (1 John 3:7, NIV).

Deceivers were abundant in John's day, so believers frequently needed to be alerted to the dangers of deception. No deception could be more insidious than an empty claim to righteousness that was not confirmed by an evident practice of right living. John wants his *"little children"* to know that the one who is righteous is the one who does that which is right, not simply the one who claims to be righteous.

The words *"is righteous"* defines the moral innocence both of the man who *"doeth righteousness"* and of God Himself! God's righteousness is absolute — there is no darkness at all to degrade His character. So the disciple who is under the blood of Christ is as righteous as God is righteous. John does not claim that the believer's performance is perfectly upright and forever sinless. He sees the Christian as one who has *"Jesus Christ, the righteous One"* (1 John 2:1) and as one who goes before God as his *" Advocate"* to defend and become *"propitiation"* to satisfy God when he does sin. John declares such a believer *"righteous"* (1 John 1:7; 2:2). Whatever actual *"righteousness"* the Christian possesses is accredited to him because of his faith in and obedience to Christ.

> *He that doeth sin is of the devil: for the devil sinneth from the beginning. To this end was the son of God manifested, that he might destroy the works of the devil* (1 John 3:8, ASV). *He who does what is sinful is of the devil, because the devil has been sinning from the beginning. The reason the Son of God appeared was to destroy the devil's work* (1 John 3:8, NIV).

The devil is a career sinner and the instigator of all sin. He started the rebellion against morality. Then He got man involved in the conspiracy — *"He was a murderer from the beginning, not holding to the truth, for there is no truth in him. When he lies, he speaks his native language, for he is a liar and the father of lies"* (John 8:44). John's point is not that Satan has sinned but that he **is sinning** — his whole existence is sin.

Just as surely as the one who keeps on doing righteousness is of God, so also the one who keeps on doing sin is of the devil. A person's settled practice, whether it is righteousness or sinful, establishes his spiritual identity with God or with Satan.

The phrase *"of the devil"* is a genitive prepositional phrase that establishes the father/child relationship. There is a "like father, like son" syndrome at work in this verse and 1 John 3:7. 1 John 3:10 is still part of the children of God and children of the devil manifestation.

The phrase *"to destroy the devil's work"* contains the **third,** and definitely the most urgent, **reason** for the mission of Jesus to be added to those in 1 John 3:5. Satan's *"works"* are sins. Christ's mission was to *"destroy"* (***luse***) which means to loose or to finish by unloosing the Devil's work. Jesus literally came to terminate sin's grip on mankind by His atoning sacrifice. Sin no longer *"has dominion"* over the disciple (Romans 6:14, ASV). It was through the cross that he *"took away sin"* (1 John 3:5; cf. Hebrews 2:14-15).

> *Whosoever is begotten of God doeth no sin, because his seed abideth in him: and he cannot sin, because he is begotten of God* (1 John 3:9, ASV). *No one who is born of God will continue to sin, because God's seed remains in him; he cannot go on sinning, because he has been born of God* (1 John 3:9, NIV).

"Whosoever is begotten of God" relates to any Christian who stands in a born-again relationship with God. The perfect tense *"is begotten"* defines the present linear result of the past birth process. John does not discuss someone who **was** *"born"* in the past without any definition of his present practice. He is dealing only with the man who *"**is** begotten/ is born of God,"* who presently has a standing new birth. *"Doeth* (***poiei***) is a present, active, auxiliary verb that defines a practice **and** an ongoing process.

The words *"He cannot sin"* insist that such a person cannot go on sinning because that is the impact of the present active infinitive *"cannot sin"* (***ou' dunatai hamartanein***). Anyone *"abiding in God"* (1 John 3:6) and who *"is begotten of God"* cannot have a present practice of sin because the two conditions cannot simultaneously co-exist. Just as *"light"* and *"darkness"* are mutually exclusive, so the practice of sin and a standing new birth relation are impossible combinations. Remember that a standing practice of sin is *"walking in darkness,"* and that makes any claim to fellowship with God *"a lie"* (1 John 1:6)! If one who *"is begotten of God"* were to cease the practice of *"righteousness"* (1 John 3:6) and begin a practice of *"sin,"* he would lose his standing new birth and would find himself in the relationship with the devil as defined in 1 John 3:9. To live like the devil precludes the new birth either in its reception or in its progression (cf. 1 John 3:8). Repentance from the practice of sin is prerequisite to the new birth and a penitent life-style is prerequisite to keeping the new birth intact.

John is an absolutist! A man cannot have an on-going new birth relationship with God and at the same time have an on-going sinful identity with the Devil. He is not denying that a Christian cannot sin because that would contradict what he so pointedly affirmed in 1 John 1 and 2. He simply says that the new birth and the practice of sin cannot co-exist.

The fact that God's seed abides in the Christian becomes the rationale for John's affirmation that such a man cannot sin. The *"seed"* (**sperma**) in the New Testament consistently points to *"imperishable seed . . . the word of the Lord"* (1 Peter 1:23-25) which is the **source** of the new birth. When Jesus told the parable of the sower, He said, *"The seed is the word of God"* (Luke 8:11). Jesus explained, *"When trouble or persecution comes because of the world, . . . the worries of this life and the deceitfulness of wealth* **choke** *it* (the Word of God), *making it unfruitful"* (Matthew 13:21-22). The Lord also said, *"If you hold to my teaching, you are really my disciples. Then you will know the truth, and the truth will set you free"* (John 8:31-32). When *"God's seed remains in him* (the Christian), that is what enables him to *"walk in the light"* (1 John 1:7, 3:9). The tense for *"remains/abideth"* is present indicative. The *"seed"* acts as the constant guide for the Christian's life. The new birth is forfeited when God's *"seed"* is choked out and the Christian is no longer governed by the Word. If he begins practicing sin, he is a lawless renegade from God's standards. There is no way his new birth relationship with God will stand! He just moved himself back under the condition of being *"of the devil"* (1 John 3:8).

> *In this the children of God are manifest, and the children of the devil: whosoever doeth not righteousness is not of God, neither he that loveth not his brother* (1 John 3:10,

ASV). *This is how we know who the children of God are and who the children of the devil are: Anyone who does not do what is right is not a child of God; nor is anyone who does not love his brother* (1 John 3:10, NIV).

The words *"In this"* speak of two essential qualities by which God's people are identified: the practice of righteousness and of love. Of course, the absence of those qualities identifies the devil's victims. *"In this"* is a transitional phrase moving John's argument from the *"practice of righteousness"* to the *"love"* element as a further distinguishing factor between *"the children of God"* and the *"children of the devil."* The *"of"* related either to God or the devil is the genitive of possession, and thus defines one's spiritual parentage. God and Satan are eternally hostile one toward the other. Marcus Dobbs says, "Truth and falsehood, good and evil, right and wrong, God and the devil are irreconcilable opposites." The life-styles of their respective *"children"* are also irreconcilable opposites.

Those *"begotten of God"* are *"children of God."* As for those who are called *"children of the devil,"* John does not discuss a birth process. The devil never created anyone nor generated life in any creature, but he who lives in sin like the devil is as much a *"child of the devil"* as if Satan had actually created him! At least they are the *"children of the devil"* in much the same way that Jesus said of the Pharisees: *"You belong to your father, the devil, and you carry out your father's desire"* (John 8:44; cf. *son of the devil"* in Acts 13:10 and *"sons of the evil one"* in Matthew 13:38).

There is no neutral ground in John's dual classification. Every man is identified by his practice as to his parentage. Jesus insisted on the principle that a tree, good or bad, is known by its fruits, good or bad! (cf. Matthew 12:33). Failure to be righteous is an evil fruit that identifies a wicked tree. Likewise, failure to love the brethren exposes a man's parent connection with the devil.

APPLICATION

Some modern theologians attribute John's words in this context to the idea of the **"perseverance of the elect"** (otherwise known as the doctrine of "once saved always saved"). When John says, *"whosoever **is** begotten of God,"* that is not the same as saying, "whosoever <u>was</u> begotten of God." The *"**is** begotten"* defines what now exists as a present, remaining result of the past new birth process. According to John that present result can remain only as long as there is a present, settled practice of *"righteousness."* "<u>Was</u> *begotten*" defines an event that occurred in the past, but it does not indicate whether or not that past birth is still intact. We must conclude that a standing new birth can exist only where there is a concurrent standing practice of righteousness. And where there is a standing practice of sin, there can be no standing new birth relationship with God. It is impossible to continue the practice of sin because it cancels the new birth standing. Christians must remember that salvation is not an isolated event from the past. It is a process that exists only if one *"be faithful, **even to/unto** (unto = **axri** = until the time of) the point of death"* (Revelation 2:10; cf. Revelation 2:25-26). Therefore, Christians must be diligent to keep habitual sin from their lives. This whole context insists that the mission of Christ was to remove the guilt of sin for believers, but also to eradicate the practice of sin from their lives.

Fellowship Is Rooted
In The Practice Of Sacrificial Love

1 John 3:11-24

For this is the message which ye heard from the beginning, that we should love one another (1 John 3: 11, ASV). *This is the message you heard from the beginning: We should love one another* (1 John 3:11, NIV).

The words *"the message"* relate back to John's *"love"* discussion in 1 John 2:7-11. Clearly he considers that *"love of the brethren"* is all wrapped up in *"doing righteousness."* Fraternal affection among God's people was fixed by Christ as one of the identifying characteristics that manifest their discipleship (cf. John 13:34-35). The *"love"* (**agape**) Jesus assigned in this *"new commandment"* has a five-fold quality and requires attitudes that only a Christian can understand and practice. To *"love"* in *"new commandment"* fashion is:

1) To seek the other person's highest good.
2) To do so regardless of how much sacrifice it may cost the lover, even to the point of death.
3) To love whether the one loved deserves It or not.
4) To love whether the one loved asks for it or not. Love always volunteers and is alert to opportunities for service.
5) And to love regardless of how many times a loving act may need to be repeated.

That is just the nature of God's *"love"* for us and of Jesus' willing, sacrificial *"love"* on our behalf.

The words *"one another"* (**allelous**) are a reciprocating pronoun that defines the mutual obligation of *"love"* within the entire family of God. Evidently the term *"brother"* (**adelphon**) is an extension of John's discussion about *"the children of God"* (1 John 3:1-2, 7, 10). For the Greeks, a *"brother"* was one who came from the same womb (Thayer). In 1 John the figurative womb of new birth is a common belief in Jesus (cf. 1 John 5:1), a mutual *"love"* for the brethren (cf. 1 John 4:7), and a general practice of righteousness (cf. 1 John 3:9).

Not as Cain was of the evil one, and slew his brother. And wherefore slew he him? Because his works were evil, and his brother's righteous (1 John 3:12, ASV). Do not be like Cain, who belonged to the evil one and murdered his brother. And why did he murder him? Because his own actions were evil and his brother's were righteous (1 John 3:12, NIV).

It is interesting that John should use Cain as an example of how **not** to love. He *"slew"* (***esphaxen*** = to butcher, to slaughter) his brother Abel (cf. Genesis 4:8, 25). There are two possible reasons for the introduction of Cain into this context. First, there is the sheer contrast between Cain's killing Abel motivated by devilish jealousy and Christ's dying for His brothers motivated by divine love. The contrast is as classical as it is relevant. Second, there is a remote possibility, suggested by some commentaries, that John is taking to task a gnostic sect called the Ophites. They were associated with a bizarre form of Satan worship. They held Satan to be the hero of the temptation story in the Garden of Eden. Because they placed such a premium on knowledge, they accused God of deliberately depriving Adam and Eve of ***gnosis*** (knowledge) by forbidding the fruit of the tree of knowledge of good and evil. Admittedly, such a connection would be remote, but it does show some of the more sensational incongruities (absurd ideas, Ed.) of Gnosticism.

The syntax of 1 John 3:11 does not mesh well with the following verse. The sentence appears to have a part missing. Maybe John is saying, *"We should love one another"* **but** *"Do not be like Cain"* in the way that he showed love to his brother. Cain was a lover of sorts — he was even a sacrificial lover! He loved himself so much that when Abel became a "bother," Cain proceeded to eliminate the "bother"! Cain's love was so centered on self, that Abel's life was a meaningless object of hateful hostility. What a contrast between Christ and Cain!

John asks the question *"And why did he murder him?"* seeking the motive behind the action which is always an important consideration. It appears that Cain's jealousy over God's approval of Abel's sacrifice was the root of his deed. John already stated that *"Cain was of the evil one,"* but Satan was behind the dastardly deed. Cain's actions were not the result of an isolated temper tantrum. The murderous act was indeed an isolated action, but it was also a display of a settled life-style. Cain's *"works were evil"* and the slaughter of Abel was but one example of habitual wickedness. On the other hand, Abel's life pattern illustrated his righteous way of life.

Marvel not, brethren, if the world hateth you (1 John 3:13, ASV). *Do not be surprised, my brothers, if the world hates you* (1 John 3:13, NIV).

There is a divinely imposed hostility between good and evil. In the Garden of Eden, God told Satan in the presence of Adam and Eve, *"I will put enmity between you and the woman, and between your offspring and hers; . . .* (Genesis 3:15). God does not want good and evil to co-exist in peaceful harmony. He placed the animosity between the two, and He wants His people to expect the opposition of those on the devil's side. Cain is an enduring example of the natural antagonism between good and evil. Any tolerance or harmony between light and darkness confuses both saints and sinners. It definitely blurs God's standards.

Those who practice righteousness become the natural objects of the world's hostility. Jesus explained, *"Everyone who does evil hates the light, and will not come into the light for fear that his deeds will be exposed"* (John 3:20). Christians should not be distressed when the world hates them for that just proves they are not a part of the world. Jesus comforted his people in such matters, saying,

If you belonged to the world, it would love you as its own. As it is, you do not belong to the world, but I have chosen you out of the world. That is why the world hates you (John 15:19). *We know that we have passed out of death into life, because we love the brethren. He that loveth not abideth in death* (1 John 3:14, ASV). *We know that we have passed from death to life, because we love our brothers. Anyone who does not love remains in death* (1 John 3:14, NIV).

Even if the world hates the Christians, *"we know"* that our relationship with God is genuine. John's repetition is emphatic in merit, for *"we"* — *"we know that we have passed."* The word *"passed"* (**metabebekamen** = stepped over; out of) speaks of the transition from spiritual *"death into life"* and this is where we remain alive. Such is the impact of the perfect tense verb. To *"pass ...from death to life"* is the best definition of what happens when one is *"born again"* (John 3:3, 7). John says the evidence that the transition has taken place is *"because we love the brethren."*

In the Gospel of John, Jesus describes those who have been a part of the *"new birth"* as one who *"hears my word and believes him who sent me."* This kind of man *"has eternal life and will not be condemned; he has crossed over from death to life"* (John 5:24). Paul discusses the same event, *"For he has rescued us from the dominion of darkness and brought us into the kingdom of the Son he loves"* (Colossians 1:13).

The phrase *"He that loveth not abideth in death"* affirms that a present failure to love produces a present residence in spiritual death. To love not is to live not!

Whosoever hateth his brother is a murderer: and ye know that no murderer hath eternal life abiding in him (1 John 3:15, ASV). *Anyone who hates his brother is a murderer, and you know that no murderer has eternal life in him* (1 John 3:15, NIV).

Cain is brought into the picture again to establish that *"hate"* not only destroys the life of others, it destroys the possibility of *"eternal life"* for the hater! There is no ground of salvation on a platform of hate, because it is the motive for murder. God told Cain, even before the overt deed was done that because of his mood *"sin is crouching at your door; it desires to have you, but you must master it"* (Genesis 4:7).

Jesus insisted that the motives behind sinful actions bring the same degree of guilt as does the sinful deed itself (cf. Matthew 5:22-23, 27). The sin hurts those sinned against, but the motive hurts the one committing the sin.

The words *"you know"* state a self-evident truth that *"fellowship with God"* cannot arise from a base of evil sentiments toward others. *"Eternal life"* cannot *"abide"* where *"hate abides."* As *"love"* in 1 John 3:14 is evidence of *"life,"* so *"hate"* in verse 15 is evidence of *"death!"*

> ***Hereby*** *know we love, because he laid down his life for us: and we ought to lay down our lives for the brethren* (1 John 3:16, ASV) [Emphasis added]. *This is how we know what love is: Jesus Christ laid down his life for us. And we ought to lay down our lives for our brothers* (1 John 3:16, NIV).

Thirteen times John echoes *"hereby"* (***en touto*** = in this) to give his readers evidence about things *"we know"* to be true. Most of the times, his *"hereby"* statements are made to reassure the Christian of his standing before God (cf. 1 John 2:3, 5; 3:10, 16, 19, 24; 4:2, 6, 9, 10, 13, 17; 5:2). In this verse the *"hereby"* points to the practical definition of *"love."*

The transition from *"hate"* to *"love"* offers John an opportunity to define authentic *"love."* Real *"love"* (***agape***) finds its greatest expression, and in fact, its only genuine manifestation, in what Christ did for us. In sacred history there have been many inspiring episodes of sacrificial love for God or for a friend. But what Jesus did is so unique that John makes it the standard by which the ***agape*** quality of love is best defined. Without the sacrificial *"love"* of Jesus, the world would be deprived of the true revelation of the essence of *"love."*

The phrase *"He laid down his life for us"* explains what *"love"* is all about. *"For"* (***huper***) makes His laying down His life a vicarious, substitutionary act. *"He laid down his life"* makes the act voluntary, deliberate, and intentional. Jesus said:

> *I lay down my life — only to take it up again. No one takes if from me, but I lay it down of my own accord. I*

have authority to lay it down and authority to take it up again (John 10:17-18).

Jesus' sacrifice was motivated by *"love,"* because *"greater love has no one than this, that he lay down his life for his friends"* (John 15:13). *"Lay down"* is the same language John used about the action of Jesus in the upper room, when he casually *"laid aside"* His garments (cf. John 13:4) and washed the Apostle's feet. The *"laid down his life"* was far from casual even if the same root words are used to define the act. The unworthiness of the *"us"* for whom Jesus died gives nobility to His sacrifice, because the *"us"* did not deserve such sacrificial devotion. In fact, we deserved the opposite. Remember that we are the *"morally weak, sinning, ungodly enemies"* of Romans 5:5-8!

A student in a class I was teaching related an episode that occurred in his life that gives deeper appreciation for the sacrifice of Jesus. He and some of his fellow soldiers were under heavy enemy fire; they hastily dug a fox-hole in which to bury themselves. When an unpinned enemy hand grenade was thrown into their bunker, one of the soldiers voluntarily covered the grenade with his body just as it exploded. That soldier saved the lives of his colleagues in arms at the cost of his own life. When asked how he felt about the sacrifice of his buddy, the surviving soldier replied: "How should I feel? There I was, alive, but covered with his blood." Without any attempt to diminish the virtue of that event, it must be remembered that Jesus' sacrifice separates itself from that battlefield experience in several significant ways. Only if the same soldier had fallen on a grenade that menaced a group of enemy soldiers would his act approach the borders of what Jesus did for His enemies. The symbolic grenade that menaced our spiritual lives was not a man-made bomb; it was the sins we committed. The threat of death was not simply physical, but spiritual and eternal. Jesus allowed the *"sword"* of divine justice to strike Him (as our Shepherd) for the sins of His sheep (cf. Zechariah 13:7). Because of the Shepherd, the sheep are alive, covered with *"his blood"* (Ephesians 1:7).

"And we ought to lay down our lives for our brothers" — the *"and"* unites His sacrifice for us with our duty of sacrificial *"love for our brothers." "Ought"* (***opheilei*** = debt or obligation) places every Christian who has been redeemed under the moral duty to *"lay down our lives"* for other Christians. The last full measure of devotion is what the new commandment demands of us all. We may not feel that *"our brothers"* **deserve** our sacrifice, but neither did we **deserve** the sacrifice of Jesus. Therefore, any brother or sister in Christ that was on Jesus' love-list when He went to the cross must also be on our love-list!

APPLICATION

If the church can be this sacrificially concerned for those in the church family, that will go far in attracting the attention of those outside the family. Jesus promised, *"By this all men will know that you are my disciples, if you love one another"* (John 13:35). Of course, laying *"down our lives for our brothers"* has no atoning value as did Jesus' sacrifice, but it does manifest the sincerity of our devotion to God's family and to family duties.

> *But whoso hath the world's goods, and beholdeth his brother in need, and shutteth up his compassion from him, how doth the love of God abide in him?* (1 John 3:17, ASV). *If anyone has material possessions and sees his brother in need but has no pity on him, how can the love of God be in him?* (1 John 3:17, NIV).

The words *"the world's goods"* (***bios tou kosmou***) stand for the necessities of life or livelihood. The woman who had been subject to bleeding for twelves years *"had spent all her living* (***bios***) *on physicians"* to no avail (Luke 8:43). Because of the cross, each Christian owes his life to every other Christian as 1 John 3:16 demands. John presents the absurd inconsistency of one who owes his life to a fellow Christian, but who will not share with him a little food from his storehouse! He asks, *"How can the love of God* *be in him?"* The rhetorical question answers itself! There simply is no love for the brother! Then what feelings does the brother have who is derelict before his duty? Maybe John wants his readers to see that the absence of Christ-like *"love"* is akin to Cain-like *"hate."* Cain's <u>active aggression</u> toward Abel may not be too far removed from the *"**bios**-possessing"* brother's <u>passive neglect</u> of the needy victim. He who *"sees his brother in need and has no pity on him"* does not have Christ like *"love."*

The words *"in need"* (***xreian exonta*** = need having) are a present participle which defines a visible case of extended need. Perhaps the needy brother is literally starving. James presents a similar case where the one with the resources faces an evident urgency in his brother's need, so he offers good words but really does not help (cf. James 2:15-19).

The phrase ***"shutteth (kleisei)** up his compassion from him"* carries the impact of one slamming the door in the face of a needy brother. *"Compassion/pity"* (***splagxna*** = bowels) has to do with deep feelings. The Hebrews considered the "bowels" as the seat of emotions because of the feeling the flow of adrenaline produces in the pit of the stomach when one is exposed to pathetic situations. In John's example, there is a total absence of emotional stirring upon seeing the needs of a starving brother! How unlike Christ!

> *My little children, let us not love in word, neither with the tongue: but in deed and truth* (1 John 3:18, ASV). *Dear children, let us not love with words or tongue but with actions and in truth* (1 John 3:18, NIV).

W. Robertson Nicoll properly points out John's transition from the instrumental dative *"with"* words and *"with"* the tongue to the propositional *"**in** deeds and **in** truth."* The impact is away from empty words to tangible assistance. There are many Christians who love with words only. Charity that is only verbal is hypocritical, for it expresses agreement with the concept of ***agape,*** but it neglects the practice of *"love."* It is easy to give "lip-service" to *"love,"* but it demands devotions parallel to the *"new* *commandment"* to practice it.

The phrase *"but in deed and truth"* is really the only way true love can be manifested. *"Love"* cannot be passive before need and still qualify for the title of *"love."* Like James' *"faith without works is dead"* (James 2:26), so John's *"love"* without *"deeds"* is really equal to *"hate."* *"Love"* is often considered as a simple human emotion and indeed it is that. But the *"new commandment"* type *"love"* is an emotion that invests itself in affectionate and voluntary service. In the final analysis, this *"agape/love"* is a verb. Therefore, its assignments can be commanded by God.

The *"in deed"* part involves *"love"* in action. Clearly in this case actions speak louder than words. The *"in truth"* part must involve the motives. Jesus severely criticized the Pharisees who blew their trumpets to make a show of charity. Their motives were as empty as their claim to piety! They actually exploited the beggars to be able *"to be seen of men"* in their pretense of charity. Whatever applause the public gave their action is all the credit they will ever derive from it. God will not bless such vain display of pretended concern for the needy (cf. Matthew 6:1-4).

In I Corinthians 13 Paul discusses the emptiness of external expressions of charity that are void of proper Calvary motivations. He speaks of those who *"give all . . . to the poor and surrender* (their bodies) *to the flames"* (1 Corinthians 13:3). Those evidently are sterling examples of love, but Paul strips them of all true virtue when he says their actions were *"clanging cymbals"* and not really motivated by charity (1 Corinthians 13:1). Why would such a person do these things? If it was not for *"love"* of others, then it must have been for self-love. That simply is not John's *"love in truth."* Obviously, Paul is critical of the actions of love (*"deeds"*) without the proper motive (*"truth"*), while John is critical of the motive (*"truth"*) without the proper action (*"deed"*). Only those who *"love in deed* (actions) *and in truth"* (motive) are *"new commandment"* lovers.

Insisting on the sincerity of motive, Paul commands that *"Love must be sincere"* (Romans 12:9). Hypocritical love is love that uses the *"word"* and *"tongue"* only. Peter pleads, *"Now that you have purified yourselves by obeying the truth so that you have sincere love for your brothers, love one another deeply, from the heart"* (1 Peter 1:22).

> *Hereby shall we know that we are of the truth, and shall assure our <u>heart</u> before him: because if our <u>heart</u> condemn us, God is greater than our <u>heart</u>, and knoweth all things. Beloved, if our <u>heart</u> condemns us not, we have boldness toward God* (1 John 3:19-21, ASV). *This then is how we know that we belong to the truth, and how we set our <u>hearts</u> at rest in his presence whenever our <u>hearts</u> condemn us. For God is greater than our <u>hearts</u>, and he knows everything. Dear friends, if our <u>hearts</u> do not condemn us, we have confidence before God* (1 John 3:19-21, NIV).

These three verses must be studied together because they contain a common message about the Christian's conscience. John speaks of the *"heart"* four times in the context. Notice first that John wants us to *"set our hearts at rest . . . whenever our hearts condemn us."* An *"assured . . . heart"* is based on the fact that *"God is greater than our hearts, and he knows everything."* When God over rules our *"heart"* (the heart that condemns us), our heart can no longer condemn us.

The conscience is that God-given faculty that monitors all our actions and either *"accuses"* the wrong or *"defends"* the right deeds (cf. Romans 2:15). When we do not measure up to the standard of *"love"* (cf. 1 John 3:16) our heart condemns us. We agree with the duty of love and are committed to the practice of it, but often feel guilty because we have not loved as we *"ought."* John does not want Christians to feel lost even when they feel guilty for occasional lapses in their *"love"* assignment. Thank God! Our eternal destiny is not determined by the condemning judgment of our own accusing conscience.

The Christian has reason to be *"assured"* even when his conscience condemns him for the simple fact, as John presents it, that *"God is greater than our hearts."* The greatness of God as our judge is the source of our assurance. Our conscience functions as a **local court** that condemns each failure of *"love."* But John presents God as a **higher court** that over-rules the judgments of the local court judge (representing our conscience/heart). It is God who pronounces an acquittal. God does over-rule the judgment of our conscience simply because our conscience does condemn the failure! We would really be in trouble if our conscience did not condemn our failures. The thoughts John expresses here are basically what he presented in 1 John 1:9: *"If we confess our sins, he is faithful and just and will forgive us our sins and purify us from all unrighteousness."* In our confession of sins, we agree with God's assessment and acknowledge our failures.

John comforts us by saying, *"God is greater than our hearts, and he knows everything."* He knows our desire to practice the love-standard. He knows our regret for failure, sees our intention to do better, and He gives us credit for our intentions.

> *Beloved, if our heart condemn us not, we have boldness toward God; and whatsoever we ask we receive of him, because we keep his commandments and do the things that are pleasing to him* (1 John 3:21-22, ASV). *Dear friends, if our hearts do not condemn us, we have confidence before God and receive from him anything we ask, because we obey his commands and do what pleases him* (1 John 3:21-22, NIV).

The only person who can properly have a heart that does not condemn is the Christian whose sins are covered by Christ. It is the Christian's *"walk in the light"* that allows *"the blood of Jesus, his Son, to purify us from all sin"* (1 John 1:7). Such a man is at peace with God, and stands with an *"assured . . . heart before him."*

The phrase *"we have boldness"* (**parresian**) speaks of the confident freedom of speech in our communication with God. If we know that we are in such a state of grace before God, then our prayer life is enhanced and emboldened. Christians stand as beloved children before their provident Father. They do not stand in fear as a sinner accused before an awful judge. The *"boldness/confidence"* with which we ask is balanced with the confidence of receiving the answer to our prayer. Greater attention to "asking" and "receiving" will be given in 1 John 5:14-17.

The **two reasons** given for confidence in receiving what we asked of God may appear analogous (similar) in content. John says we receive *"because we obey his commands and do what pleases him."* This is present active indicative which really defines the Christian's consistent walk even as Jesus walked (cf. 1 John 2:6). *"And do"* (**poioumen**) means we regularly practice the things that are pleasing to him. It does not mean that Christians go beyond keeping His commandments by doing other things that are pleasing to him. The **first** reason for the Christian's confidence is obedient submission to commanded standards. The **second** reason possibly touches on the loving motives behind keeping His commandments. The first reason is **observing** God's law; the second is **loving** God's law.

> *And this is his commandment, that we should believe in the name of his son Jesus Christ, and love one another, even as he gave us commandment* (1 John 3:23, ASV). *And this is his command: to believe in the name of his Son, Jesus Christ, and to love one another as he commands us* (1 John 3:23, NIV).

If belief is a personal conviction, and love is a personal emotion, how can God command either one? Belief is a response to verifiable evidence. When God gives adequate evidence for Himself, He has a right to demand that men evaluate the evidence and come to faith. To refuse to believe in the face of manifest evidence is to stand before God *"without excuse"* for the unbelief (cf. Romans 1:20). God can command *"love"* because it is a response to the captivating love of God that was demonstrated in creation and in recreation — *"We love because he first loved us"* (1 John 4:19) — since *"love"* is also a verb, God can command the action that manifests it.

> *And he that keepeth his commandments abideth in him,*
> *and he in him. And hereby we know that he abideth in us,*
> *by his spirit which he gave us* (1 John 3:24, ASV). *Those*
> *who obey his commands live in him, and he in them. And*
> *this is how we know that he lives in us: We know it by the*
> *Spirit he gave us* (1 John 3:24, NIV).

Consistent **commandment keeping** is John's verifiable
evidence that God abides in us and we abide in him. Such unity
and mutual residence between God and believers is simply another
definition of fellowship. Remember that any claim to *"know"* God
is exposed as a lie if the claimant does not keep His
commandments (cf. 1 John 2:4).

The words *"And hereby we know"* are John's offer of
evidence that the Christian and God have fellowship. The evidence
is the indwelling *"Spirit which he gave us."* Without controversy,
the presence of the *"Spirit"* confirms redemption and is evidence
of it (cf. Romans 8:9, 14-15). But how does one know whether the
"Spirit" indwells him? He knows it by divine promise and
revelation — the promise was given in Acts 2:38-39 and the
revelation is through apostolic witness in Acts 5:32, Galatians 4:6,
Ephesians 1:14-15, and 1 John 4:13-15.

APPLICATION

There has never been greater demands placed on Christians of
all ages than their assignment to *"love."* It conditions their
obedience to God's commands. It makes noble their interaction
and fellowship with their brethren. Its absence is so strident in its
contrast with the cross of Jesus. But its presence is the Christians
most winsome quality. It is easy to subscribe to the beauty of
Christ's loving example and even to give verbal praise because of
it. His loving sacrifice demanded that he *"empty himself"* of all
privileges of deity and to *"humble himself"* in human surrender to

the cross (cf. Philippians 2:5-10). So the *"love"* assignment He gave makes no less demand of us today. We bow to the virtue of *"love,"* therefore, we must bow to the sacrificial service of *"love."* It has been said that we should not tell anyone that "Jesus loves you" until we are ready to do for them what Jesus' love demands of us.

The First Epistle of John

Fellowship Is Rooted In The Rejection Of False Doctrine

1 John 4:1-6

Beloved, believe not every spirit, but prove the spirits, whether they are of God; because many false prophets are gone out into the world (1 John 4:1, ASV). *Dear friends, do not believe every spirit, but test the spirits to see whether they are from God, because many false prophets have gone out into the world* (1 John 4:1, NIV).

The word *"Beloved"* is an affectionate address (cf. 1 John 4:7, 11). Evidently, John wants to confirm his love for those he calls *"my little children."* He has urgent warnings to give them, but first he must assure them that his concern for their loyalty to apostolic truth does not diminish his tender devotion for them.

John begins with *"believe not"* which is a present indicative imperative command. It **insists** that they stop believing the false prophets. Apparently, gnostic teachers were making some inroads into the church's doctrinal positions about Jesus Christ.

Gnostics loved to call themselves "spirit" people because that term separated them from those uninitiated in gnostic doctrine whom they called "flesh" people. John applies their "spirit" terminology to *"every"* teacher who would instruct God's people. Some *"spirits"* are exposed as *"false prophets"* while others are affirmed as being *"of God."* John expands on the menace posed by the *"antichrists"* he has already discussed (cf. 1 John 2:18).

With his command to *"prove/test"* (**dokimazete**), which is the method by which metal is assayed (cf. Proverbs 17:3), John insists that *"every"* teacher be tested. The imperative command to stop believing the spirits is united with another equally urgent imperative command to *"prove the spirits."* The *"many false prophets"* are the *"spirits"* whose doctrine must be tested.

> **Hereby** *know ye the Spirit of God: every spirit that confesseth that Jesus Christ is come in the flesh is of God* (1 John 4:2, ASV) [Emphasis added]. *This is how you can recognize the Spirit of God: Every spirit that acknowledges that Jesus Christ has come in the flesh is from God,* (1 John 4:2, NIV).

The phrase *"This is how you can recognize"* introduces the doctrinal criteria by which the *"spirits"* are to be evaluated. God has His spokesmen, but first they must be identified. *"The spirit of God"* is not a reference to the Holy Spirit, because John had just mentioned the Holy Spirit (cf. 1 John 3:24). The word *"spirit"* should not be capitalized because John speaks of *"every spirit . . . is from God,"* which implies a plurality of *"spirits"* under discussion and there is only one Holy Spirit.

The *"little children"* must be able to distinguish between teachers of truth and those who propagate error. John proceeds to separate *"every spirit"* (teacher) that is *"of God"* in this verse from *"every spirit"* that is not *"of God"* in the next verse.

God acknowledges only those who *"acknowledge that Jesus Christ has come in the flesh."* The test criteria is simple, but adequate. The test can be made by asking the teacher if Jesus left footprints when he walked in the sand. If the answer is yes, then that teacher is repeating the apostolic testimony relative to the actual humanity of Jesus. John may also include in the *"test"* a question about Jesus being the Messiah of Old Testament prophecy. If the answer is yes in both cases, that teacher is *"of God."*

The phrase *"Jesus Christ is come,"* is a perfect participle and insists that Jesus not only *"became flesh"* (cf. John 1:14), but that He also still abides *"in the flesh."* That explains why He can still *"be touched with the feelings of our infirmities"* (Hebrews 4:15, ASV). He is still *"man"* (cf. John 5:27; Acts 17:31; 1 Timothy 2:5).

> *And every spirit that confesseth not Jesus is not of God:*
> *and this is the spirit of the antichrist, whereof ye have*
> *heard that it cometh; and now it is in the world already*
> (1 John 4:3, ASV). *But every spirit that does not*
> *acknowledge Jesus is not from God. This is the spirit of*
> *the antichrist, which you have heard is coming and even*
> *now is already in the world* (1 John 4:3, NIV).

"Jesus" is the human name that was given by revelation to Joseph (cf. Matthew 1:21), so any *"spirit"* that denies the human implication of the name Jesus *"is not of God."* Jerome's Latin Vulgate translates this verse as: *"every spirit that severs Jesus is not of God."* Such men as Irenaeus, Clement of Alexandria, Origen, Tertullian, and Augustine assumed this translation was justified. As B. B. Wescott explains the implication is that Cerinthian Gnosticism attempted to separate the divine from the human, dividing the one divine-human Person. Further inference from the Vulgate translation may involve the separation of the man Jesus from His Messianic roots in the Old Testament. Since there is not a single Greek manuscript that carries the Vulgate reading, it is not authentic and is to be rejected. However, the fact that those early post-apostolic writers acknowledged such a variation stands to prove just how "anti-Christian" the theology of the *"antichrist"* was.

At any rate, John explains that the denial of Jesus' humanity and divinity is the heart and core of the antichrist's teachings — *"this is the spirit of antichrist."* The word *"spirit"* is not in the original text, but its import is strongly implied. The neuter singular article before the word *"spirit"* gives a construction something akin to: *"this is <u>the thing</u> of antichrist."* Denying the humanity of

Jesus is the identifying mark, the fundamental characteristic of Gnosticism, and the backbone of their theology.

> *Ye are of God, my little children, and have over come them: because greater is he that is in you than he that is in the world* (1 John4:4, ASV). *You, dear children, are from God and have overcome them, because the one who is in you is greater than the one who is in the world* (1 John 4:4, NIV).

The phrase *"You, dear children, are from God"* reconfirms the spiritual union John's *"little children"* have with God. *"Have overcome them,"* being a present perfect verb, assures the *"little children"* of lasting victory over Gnostic error and *"because greater is he that is in you"* explains the **source** of their success over gnostic teachers. It is God — *"He that is in you"* must be God. He is the One who *"abides in Christians and in whom they abide"* (1 John 3:24, ASV). *"He that is in them"* is patently Satan — the *"prince of this world"* (John 12:31) and *"the god of this age"* (2 Corinthians 4:4). The primary root of all false doctrine is:

> *The ruler of the kingdom of the air, the spirit who is now at work in those who are disobedient/ prince of the powers of the air, of the spirit that now worketh in the sons of disobedience* (Ephesians 2:2).

The word *"overcome"* translates for John into a Christian's victory. He mentions Christ's victory over Satan (cf. John 16:33), His present triumph at God's right hand (cf. Revelation 12:11), and then shows how Christians share in Jesus' victories (cf. Revelation 2:7; 21:7).

> *They are of the world: therefore speak they as of the world, and the world heareth them* (1 John 4:5, ASV). *They are from the world and therefore speak from the viewpoint of the world, and the world listens to them* (1

John 4:5, NIV).

The phrase *"They are of the world"* identifies those who *"do not confess that Jesus is come in the flesh."* Their epistemology is worldly in origin. Paul classified the same gnostic teachers of his day as promoting *"hollow and deceptive philosophy, which depends on human tradition/**tradition of men** and the basic principles of this world /**rudiments of the world** rather than on Christ"* (Colossians 2:8). He further identified some of their doctrines as self imposed with *"false humility and the worship of angels . . . such a person goes into great detail about what he has seen, and his unspiritual mind puffs him up with idle notions. He has lost connection with the Head"* (Colossians 2:18-19). ***"Traditions of men"*** are simple human speculation. ***"Rudiments"*** (***stoixeia***) form the a-b-cs of so-called human wisdom. These men saw visions and discussed them in great detail. Their *"unspiritual/fleshly mind"* feeds a boastful ego that is *"vainly puffed up"* beyond reason. They speak with the world's viewpoint because that is the source of the pretended knowledge of those who invent their own philosophy and theology.

The phrase *"and the world listens to them"* suggests that the world is a willing audience to gnostic teachers. The truth always suffers when false teachers present enticing doctrines that nourish human pride and teach a relative morality. Paul told Timothy:

> *For the time will come when men will not put up with sound doctrine. Instead, to suit their own desires, they will gather around them a great number of teachers to say what their itching ears want to hear. They will turn their ears away from the truth and turn aside to myths* (2 Timothy 4:3-4).

John sees the same menacing process at work in the world of his day.

We are of God: he that knoweth God heareth us; he who

is not of God heareth us not. By this we know the Spirit of truth, and the spirit of error (1 John 4:6, ASV). *We are from God, and whoever knows God listens to us; but whoever is not from God does not listen to us. This is how we recognize the Spirit of truth and the spirit of falsehood* (1 John 4:6, NIV).

The *"we"* and *"us"* of this verse refers to the apostolic college. John identifies the true believers as being *"of God"* and placed them in sharp contrast to gnostic followers (cf. 1 John 4:4). In this verse he expands the *"of God"* identification to include the Apostles, and thus maintain their distinction from gnostic teachers. *"They are of the world"* defines the gnostic epistemology. *"We are of God"* defines apostolic epistemology. The Apostles were God-chosen, God-appointed, and God-sent men (cf. John 15:16), therefore, their message was God-given. Just before His ascension, Jesus assured the Apostles that *"whoever accepts anyone I send accepts me; and whoever accepts me accepts the one who sent me"* (John 13:20).

John's words *"whoever knows God listens to us"* affirms that genuine knowledge about God can be obtained only from apostolic testimony. There is a clear affirmation that the Apostles have all the information about God that is needed by Christians. They are not simply the source of some knowledge about God, rather the *"anointing"* they received from Jesus *"teaches them all things"* (1 John 2:20, 27). The rejection of the Apostle's message eliminates the only valid source of theology.

The instructions to *"test the spirits"* is still a matter of concern. The options in this context are clear. The teachings are either from God or from worldly men. The hearers are indwelt either by God or by Satan. They are motivated either by an attitude of *"truth"* or by an attitude of *"error."* The lines of separation between those who follow the Apostles and those who follow the Gnostics are as distinct as those that separate heaven from hell.

There were two different groups of teachers with two different messages from two different sources that were vying for attention.

There were two opposing moods, or attitudes at work in John's day. He calls them *"the spirit of truth"* and *"the spirit of error."* *"The spirit of truth,"* and *"the spirit of error"* is determined by whose voice one follows. Clearly the Apostles witness to the truth, and those who follow their message are motivated by *"the spirit of truth."* Conversely, those whose message contradicts that which the Apostles taught are prompted by *"the spirit of error."*

APPLICATION

Teachers today who claim that "God told me this" or "God revealed that to me" are not limiting their doctrine to New Testament scripture. They are motivated by the *"spirit of error."* If their message is not found in the written Word of God, then they are to be avoided with all caution. Jude affirmed that the apostolic message was *"once for all delivered/entrusted to the saints"* (Jude 3) in the first century. It is not a product of doctrinal evolution. John assures us that the *"truth, which lives in us and will be with us forever"* (2 John 2). Peter insists that *"the word of the Lord stands forever"* (1 Peter 1:25). The standard of truth for all generations is what the Apostles and prophets gave the church in New Testament scriptures. Thus Paul imperatively commands two things of the church: *"stand firm/stand fast and hold to /hold fast to the teachings/traditions we passed on to you, whether by word of mouth or by letter"* (2 Thessalonians 2:15). What a man feels in his heart about certain doctrinal matters often carries more weight for some people than does the Word of God. Thus feelings become the final epistemology, and that is nothing short of the *"spirit of error."*

Fellowship Is Rooted in God's Love
Perfected in Practice

1 John 4:7-21

Beloved, let us love one another: for love is of God; and everyone that loveth is begotten of God, and knoweth God (1 John 4:7, ASV). *Dear friends, let us love one another, for love comes from God. Everyone who loves has been born of God and knows God* (1 John 4:7, NIV).

Those who are *"beloved"* are commanded to *"love"* others. The *"love"* John discusses has its roots, its motivations, and its practices in God. We love because He first loved us (cf. 1 John 4:19). His loving investment in us at Calvary is adequate motivation for our loving response. And it is His loving devotion to our salvation that makes noble our practice of love.

John says, *"Everyone that loveth* (present indicative) *is begotten* (present perfect) *of God."* The prerequisite to the new birth and essential fruit of that new birth is the Christian's commitment to *"love."* John has already given disclaimers to hate as a platform for the new birth (cf. 1 John 2:9; 3:14-15).

We *"know God"* because we daily bask in His *"love."* We experience the beauty of divine *"love"* both in providence and in redemption. Having tasted that God is good (cf. 1 Peter 2:3), we are animated to imitate our Father (cf. Matthew 5:43-48). This is how His love is made complete in us (cf. 1 John 2:5).

He that loveth not knoweth not God; for God is love (1 John 4:8, ASV). *Whoever does not love does not know God, because God is love* (1 John 4:8, NIV).

For some people the simple declaration of a truth does not always declare the evident error of whatever is its opposite. So John clearly states both sides for his readers. He states the positive:

"he who loves knows God." Then he reinforces that truth with the negative: *"he that loves not knows not God."*

The Gnostic claims to be intellectually elite. He holds John's *"little children"* in disdain because they reject his alleged higher knowledge. Just as *"love"* identifies those who are *"begotten of God,"* in the same manner, "not loving" exposes those who pretend to know God.

"God is (estin/is = a verb of being) *love."* This is more a definition of His nature than of His activity. Because *"God is love,"* that personifies everything He does. What He does grows out of what He is. He creates, recreates, rules, educates, admonishes, reproves, and judges — and everything He does is done in *"love."*

Since self-sacrificing *"love"* is God's essential character, then the cross of Calvary **had to be!** The statement made in 1 John 4:9 is an automatic consequence of the reality stated in 1 John 4:7. Without the cross, God's *"love"* would be without its necessary verification.

> *Herein was the love of God manifested in us, that God hath sent his only begotten Son into the world that we might live through him* (1 John 4:9, ASV). *This is how God showed his love among us: He sent his one and only Son into the world that we might live through him* (1 John 4:9, NIV).

God showed His love through the cross. This love is as natural as the sun shinning, the clouds raining, and the wind blowing. If the *"love"* John discusses is of the self-sacrificing, *agape* quality, then its manifestation has to be demonstrated. This kind of *"love"* cannot be passive in the presence of urgent needs. The manifestation is seen in the fact that God sent His Son. The *"only begotten Son"* primarily speaks of His uniqueness, but also of His preciousness to the Father. As the *"one and only Son,"* Jesus alone reproduces and reveals (*exegesato*) the nature of the Father (cf. John 1:18).

The words *"hath sent"* (**apestalken**) are a perfect active verb that defines a permanent mission the Father is accomplishing through the Son. Jesus is still fulfilling His God-sent ministry of redemption.

God's *"love manifested in us"* speaks of a *"love"* investment He made **"in us."** *"In us"* does not seem to express God's *"love"* among us or even to us. There is something inward about the Father's investment. He has made a deposit in His people. Evidently, the Father wants His <u>love-deposit</u> to produce <u>love-interest</u> from our imitation of His <u>love invested.</u> John discusses the love that God has *"in"* us again and also the profit/benefits of His love living in us (cf. 1 John 4:12-17). Properly understood and practiced, the Father's love will produce kindred fruits in the lives of Christian people.

The fruit of salvation that believers receive from God's love-investment at Calvary is living through Jesus. John explains **why** Jesus came (with a **hina/that** clause that says "in order that") when he says, *"**that** we might live through him."* God sent Jesus to receive our death sentence and to vicariously give us His life to rescue us from our death in sin (cf. Ephesians 2:1-5). The most obvious conclusion is: *"For God so loved the world"* (John 3:16) that He sent Jesus on a <u>death mission</u>. If we are to **"live,"** then **He** must die!

> *Herein is love, not that we loved God, but that he loved us, and **sent** his Son to be the **propitiation** for our sins* (1 John 4:10, ASV) [Emphasis added]. *This is love: not that we loved God, but that he loved us and **sent** his Son as an **atoning sacrifice** for our sins* (1 John 4:10, NIV) [Emphasis added].

Divine *"love"* initiated the total process of redemption even before the *"creation of the world"* (Ephesians 1:4). The verb *"sent"* (**apesteilen**) is <u>aorist tense</u> in this verse and it refers to the crucifixion as <u>an event isolated in time</u>. The <u>perfect tense</u> of Jesus being *"sent"* in 1 John 4:9 defines the <u>ongoing result of His</u>

incarnation. A. T. Robertson explains the love of God "is a conclusion from the fact He has provided in Christ, and supremely in His death, a propitiation for sins."

The phrase *"not that we loved God"* is a disclaimer that man's winsomeness or worthiness was the main reason for the redemptive mission of Jesus. There is no way man can earn or work his way to heaven. Paul is so clear when he insisted, *"But the righteousness that is by faith . . ."* (Romans 10:6) comes from divine grace and not human effort. Paul also stated that if salvation was *"by grace, it is no more of works (man's intended); otherwise grace is no more grace"* (Romans 11:6, ASV). Paul's discussion of *"grace"* and John's thoughts about *"love"* mesh into a composite of divine kindness!

The phrase *"to be the propitiation"* certainly speaks of God's saving intent behind Calvary. There is an aspect of the Father's involvement that must not escape us as benefactors of his *"love."* Remember the word *"propitiation"* carries the concept of satisfaction and appeasement of God's wrath against us for our sins. Because of His *"love,"* Christ voluntarily surrendered Himself to be the object of that wrath, thereby allowing the Father to be *"just"* before His law and at the same time to be the *"justifier"* of those who trust His atoning sacrifice (cf. Romans 3:25-26). *"God's set purpose and foreknowledge"* (Acts 2:23) made all the awful, but necessary, arrangements for our forgiveness even before we knew of the need!

> *Beloved,* ***if*** *God so loved us, we also ought to love one another* (1 John 4:11, ASV) [Emphasis added]. *Dear friends,* **since** *God so loved us, we also ought to love one another* (1 John 4:11, NIV) [Emphasis added].

"If God so loved us," then there is an essential corollary in our response. Paul said it this way — *"the love of Christ constraineth us"* (2 Corinthians 5:14, ASV) — in other words, it obligates us — Christ's love compels us to live for Him and for each other. This is the impact of John's *"we ought"* (**opheilomen**) — we are

indebted *"to love one another."* There is an additional factor at the heart of John's discourse. If God could sacrificially *"love"* us when we were sinners alienated from Him by sin, surely we can *"love one another"* now that He has made us His forgiven, *"beloved"* family. John's *"if"* speaks of reality and is equivalent with the word *"since."*

> *No man hath beheld God at any time; if we love one another, God abideth in us, and his love is perfected in us* (1 John 4:12, ASV). *No one has ever seen God; but if we love one another, God lives in us and his love is made complete in us* (1 John 4:12, NIV).

Paul's apostrophe (an exclamatory passage, Ed.) of praise is given *"Now to the King eternal, immortal, invisible, the only God be honor and glory forever and ever. Amen"* (1 Timothy 1:17). The invisible nature of our Spirit God is affirmed in John's gospel in almost identical language. *"No one has ever seen God, but God the One and Only, who is at the Father's side, has made him known"* (John 1:18, NIV). John assures his readers that *"the only begotten Son"* declares God the Father to us (John 1:18, ASV). Though God cannot be seen by man, His *"love"* for man is seen in brilliant display through His Son's sacrificial surrender on our behalf . *"God is love"* and the cross of Calvary is its supreme *"manifestation."* Just as Jesus is the living manifestation of *"life with the Father"* (1 John 1:1-4), in the same manner He is the living demonstration of the Father's *"love"* for His creation.

God's investment on Calvary results in the fruit of His *"love"* if Christians *"love one another."* Christian *"love"* for the brethren **first** confirms that God abides in us. Christians *"love"* only because *"he first loved us"* (1 John 4:19). A **second** purpose is accomplished when we love the brethren. God <u>invested a cross full of love</u> in each one of us. When His *"love"* produces a <u>cross full of love</u> in our hearts for the brethren, then, *"God's love is perfected in us."* His *"love"* is producing <u>interest on his investment.</u> One of the major purposes of Calvary, even beyond its redemptive mission, was to plant the seed of *"love"* in Christians that would produce a bountiful increase of that same kind of precious *"love"* among His children.

> *Hereby we know that we abide in him and he in us, because he hath given us of his Spirit"* (1 John 4:13, *ASV).* "We know that we live in him and he in us, *because he has given us of his Spirit* (1 John 4:13, NIV).

In chapter 4 John has given the criteria by which we know those who belong to God. On the opposite side, we can know those who are not God's children. We also know the spirit of truth and the spirit of error. In each case there are evidences that make identification simple and sure. Concerning both the new birth and the knowledge of God's nature and His abiding in us, the issue is settled by perfected *"love."* The indwelling *"gift of the Holy Spirit"* (Acts 2:38-39) assures us of what God has promised: *"'I will live with them and walk among them, and I will be their God, and they will be my people'"* (2 Corinthians 6:16). The *"gift of the Holy Spirit"* in Acts 2:38 is the genitive of identification which means the Spirit Himself is the gift. The church is the dwelling place of deity; it is the *"dwelling in which God lives by his Spirit"* (Ephesians 2:22). Thus the church is the *"temple of the Holy Spirit"* (1 Corinthians 3:16, ASV; cf. 1 John 3:24).

> *And we have beheld and bear witness that the Father hath sent the Son to be the saviour of the world* (1 John 4:14, ASV). *And we have seen and testify that the Father has sent his Son to be the Savior of the world* (1 John 4:14, NIV).

The Apostles were qualified to confirm the Father's unfolding plan for world redemption when they witnessed the death, burial, and resurrection of His Son. When John says that the Apostles *"beheld and bear witness"* in 1 John 1:1-4, he affirms the **fact** of the incarnation of Jesus. In this verse they *"beheld and bear* *witness"* to the **purpose** of the sacrifice of Jesus which was to save the world.

The word for *"beheld"* (***tetheamethe*** = as in a theater) is the same verb used in John 1:14: *"and the Word became flesh, and dwelt among us and we beheld his glory, glory as of the only begotten of the Father."* No man has *"beheld"* God, but the Apostles experienced first-hand an extended contemplation of His incarnate *"Son."*

The phrase *"to be the Savior of the world"* repeats the global redemptive mission John affirms when he includes *"the sins of the whole world"* in the propitiatory (atoning) sacrifice of our *"Advocate"* (1 John 2:2, ASV). Uniting the purpose statements made in 1 John 4:9 and 10 with this verse and the Father's commission to the Son takes on cosmic dimensions. God sent His Son so that we might live (9), and so that His Son could become the propitiation for our sins (10), and ultimately, He sent His Son so that all the world might be saved (1 John 4:9, 10, 14).

The cross of Calvary stands against the backdrop of the Father's purposes intertwined in those three verses. The bottom line of John's thought is that the *"love"* God *"manifested"* in the mission of Jesus **is redemptive!** That thought will have implications for Christians when John insists that *"God is love"* (1 John 4:16) and then draws a necessary conclusion for the church: *"as God is, even so are we in this world"* (1 John 4:17, ASV). Simply stated: **The church's mission is also redemptive!**

> *Whosoever shall confess that **Jesus is the Son of God**, God abideth in him, and he in God* (1 John 4:15, ASV) [Emphasis added]. *If anyone acknowledges that **Jesus is the Son of God**, God lives in him and he in God* (1 John 4:15, NIV) [Emphasis added].

The phrase *"Jesus is the Son of God"* unites the human *"Jesus"* with the divine *"Son of God."* John intends to leave no room for gnostic thinking about Jesus. No one may assume that a ***docetic*** (seem to be human) Jesus is a viable option to Christian faith. John insists that the Father's *"love"* has been amply *"manifested"* in the sacrifice of Jesus. But if Jesus did not have a physical body in which to suffer or physical blood to shed, where is the *"manifestation"* of the Father's *"love?"* And how could *"propitiation"* of divine wrath against sin be realized if there was no appeasing sacrifice made to God? In imitation of Jesus, we are duty bound to *"lay down our lives for our brothers"* (1 John 3:16). But if a ***docetic*** Jesus did not really *"lay down his life for us,"* there is no example for us to follow. Certainly the Gospel accounts of the Garden of Gethsemane, Pilate's judgment hall, and the crucifixion experiences are adequate to confirm the real human nature of Jesus in His struggle for world redemption.

> *And we **know** and **have believed** the love which God hath in us. God is love; and he that abideth in love abideth in God, and God abideth in him* (1 John 4:16, ASV) [Emphasis added]. *And so we **know** and **rely on** the love God has for us. God is love. Whoever lives in love lives in God, and God in him* (1 John 4:16, NIV) [Emphasis added].

The phrases *"we know"* and *"we believe"* are perfect tense verbs that define the enduring qualities of both the knowledge and the belief. To *"know"* certain historical facts is one thing; to entrust the soul's salvation to those facts is another.

The phrase *"the love which God hath in us"* again repeats the divine investment concept from 1 John 4:8. God's gift of *"love"* comes to fruition (completion) in us only when our faith in His *"love"* has led us to take possession of the salvation it offers. Beyond our salvation, God's *"love"* becomes even more fruitful when it *"is perfected in us."* Then our love for the brethren begins to take on the sacrificial flavor of Jesus.

When John says, *"God is love,"* it is not simply a definition of God's nature; it is an assignment for His people — a model for His children to imitate. John intensifies the demand God's *"love"* places on their settled practice. It is not simply *"everyone who loves"* as in 1 John 4:7, but in this verse it is *"whoever lives in love"* who has permanent residence both in God and in the practice of His *"love."* And the most glorious result is that *"he abides in God and God abides in him."* The New English Bible translates this verse, *"He who dwells in love is dwelling in God."*

> *Herein is love made **perfect** with us, that we may have boldness in the day of judgment; because as he is, even so are we in this world* (1 John 4:17, ASV) [Emphasis added]. *In this way, love is made **complete** among us so that we will have confidence on the day of judgment, because in this world we are like him* (1 John 4:17, NIV) [Emphasis added].

Perfected *"love"* in Christians exists when Calvary's love is consistently reproduced in them. God's investment in us through the cross begins to pay its dividends on a scale as wide as the brotherhood. Certainly God's *"love"* was made perfect in the sacrifice of Jesus. His *"love is made complete among us"* (**meth' hemon** = in our case) when we are sacrificially involved in the welfare of our brethren.

Another byproduct of God's vested *"love"* when it is *"made perfect"* in the church is *"boldness in the day of judgement."* *"Boldness"* (**parresian** = freedom of speech) stands in stark contrast with the *"fear"* (**phobos** = like a bond slave) of the 1 John 4:18. Such *"boldness"* is neither daring nor audacious. It simply reflects the confident assurance of those whose *"love"* response has been made noble by the imitation of Calvary's example.

Some will *"be ashamed before him at his coming"* (1 John 2:28, ASV), but others know they *"shall be like him, for we shall see him as he is"* (1 John 3:2). In view of *"the day of judgment,"* our *"love"* assignment in *"the new commandment"* must assume priority attention.

The phrase *"as he is"* has already been defined in 1 John 4:7 and 16. *"God is love,"* which is the personification of His nature and that is who we must become to be like HIM if *"as he is, so are we."* Based on conclusions properly drawn from 1 John 4:9, 10 and 14, it is evident that God's *"love"* is redemptive! God's *"love"* expresses itself in the **life giving** (1 John 4:9), **law** satisfying (1 John 4:10), and **world saving** (1 John 4:14) **mission** of *"HIS only begotten SON"* (cf. John 3:16).

Therefore, *"his love perfected in us"* must mean that the church has a mission that reflects Calvary's intent, for *"as he is, so are we."* The church must be **life-surrendering, Great Commission keeping,** and **soul seeking** in its commitment to love as He has loved.

> *There is no fear in love: but perfect love casteth out fear, because fear hath punishment: and he that feareth is not made perfect in love* (1 John 4:18, ASV) [Emphasis added]. *There is no fear in love. But perfect love drives out fear, because fear has to do with punishment. The one who fears is not made perfect in love* (1 John 4:18, NIV) [Emphasis added].

Look at the confidence John has given Christians in this epistle about our *"life with the Father and with his Son, Jesus Christ"* (1 John 1:3). We have uninterrupted *"fellowship"* between Him and us maintained by the blood of Jesus (cf. 1 John 1:7). We can know that our sins are *"forgiven"* (cf. 1 John 2:12). We have assurance that God lives in us and we abide in Him (cf. 1 John 3:24; 4:12, 16). In light of all this and more, it does not seem likely that John is speaking here of Christians with deep *"fear"* of God and dread for the coming judgment. It seems more likely that John's observations about *"fear"* and *"punishment"* would more aptly be directed toward the Gnostics who were brazen in their animosity toward the church. John knows the plight of the wicked before God: *"They called to the mountains and the rocks, 'Fall on us and hide us from the face of him who sits on the throne and from the wrath of the Lamb!'"* (Revelation 6:16). Definitely *"fear hath punishment"* even in anticipation of eternal separation from God beyond judgment (cf. Luke 16:23-28) where the *"fearful expectation of judgment and of raging fire that will consume the enemies of God"* (Hebrews 10:27). This is a literal fear. Christians who sincerely strive to *"walk as Jesus did"* (1 John 2:6) and who genuinely seek to love as Jesus loved will be present at judgment, but they will not be under judgment (cf. John 5:24). *"All who have longed for his appearing"* (2 Timothy 4:8) will stand before God with boldness and on their lips this prayer: *"Even so come, Lord Jesus"* (Revelation 22:20, ASV).

> *We **love**, because he first **loved** us* (1 John 4:19, ASV).
> *We **love** because he first **loved** us* (1 John 4:19, NIV).

The *"love"* John discusses is not native to man. It is divine in origin, in motivation, and in essential attributes. It possesses qualities that are derived only from the imitation of God's self-emptying devotion toward the undeserving.

Certain kinds of *"love"* do exist in human circles. Jesus said, *"If you love those who love you, what credit is that to you? Even 'sinners' love those who love them'"* (Luke 6:32). It takes a deeper affection than is natural to man. Jesus said:

> *Love your enemies, do good to those who hate you, bless those who curse you, pray for those who mistreat you. If someone strikes you on one cheek, turn to him the other also. If someone takes your cloak, do not stop him from taking your tunic. Give to everyone who asks you, and if anyone takes what belongs to you, do not demand it back. Do to others as you would have them do to you* (Luke 6:27-28).

This is the quality of *"love"* that God expressed toward us in sending Jesus to die in our stead.

The key word in 1 John 4:19 is ***"first."*** Whatever kinship our *"love"* expresses in selfless giving is simply a reflex action that the cross of Calvary stimulates in us. Paul is quite graphic in his description of us as the unworthy and undeserving beneficiaries of God's *"love"* both in Romans 5:6-10 and Titus 3:3-7.

Some may ask how God can command us to *"love"* since *"love"* is an emotion. True, it does involve emotions, but *"love"* also includes action and expressing verbal qualities. This verse explains that God's example of *"love"* toward us (when properly understood) makes it possible for that kind of *"love"* to become second nature with us.

> *If a man say, I love God, and hateth his brother, he is a liar: for he that loveth not his brother whom he hath seen, cannot love God whom he hath not seen* (1 John 4:20, ASV). *If anyone says, 'I love God,' yet hates his brother, he is a liar. For anyone who does not love his brother, whom he has seen, cannot love God, whom he has not seen* (1 John 4:20, NIV).

John's catch phrase to expose doctrinal, practical, or moral inconsistencies in one's religious claims is *"if a man say. . . ."* The use of the term *"brother"* is evidence that John is thinking of *"love"* within the body of believers. Failure to *"love the brethren"* makes the claim to *"love God"* an unmitigated *"lie."*

The invisibility of God is repeated (cf. 1 John 4:12). In 1 John 4:12 it is God's *"love manifested"* in Christ that is highly visible! In 1 John 4:20 it is the *"brother"* that is forever visibly present as an available object of our *"love"* assignment. The perfect tense verb *"hath seen"* indicates that the brother is always there and we can express our devotion to God by loving service to His people. We can show our love for God by the practice of God-like *"love"* toward His children.

R. W. Stott speaks of "three black lies" that John exposes. The first is **moral**: *"if we say we have fellowship with him and walk in darkness"* (1 John 1:6; 2:4). The second is **doctrinal**: *"if we say that we have the Father but deny the Son"* (1 John 2:22-23). The third is **social**: *"if we say we love God and hate our brother"* (1 John 4:20).

> *And this commandment have we from him, that he who loveth God love his brother also* (1 John 4:21, ASV). *And he has given us this command: Whoever loves God must also love his brother* (1 John 4:21, NIV).

For the second time John has tied demonstrations of *"love for his brother"* to an expression of *"love for God."* How can we show our *"love"* for God who is invisible? The answer is simply to show it by loving His children. Jesus taught that His followers could serve Him by serving the needs of His people. In fact, whatever we do for or against the disciples of Jesus, we do to Jesus Himself. When *"Saul was breathing out murderous threats against the Lord's disciples,"* Jesus took it very personally, saying, *"Saul, Saul, why do you persecute me?"* (Acts 9:1, 4). But when His followers minister to needy brethren, Jesus says, *"'I tell you the truth, whatever you did for one of the least of these brothers of mine, you did for me'"* (Matthew 25:40).

It is often regrettable that certain sections of the Bible have been broken up into chapters and verses. This in one such section. For the third time John insists that *"everyone who loves the father loves his child as well"* (1 John 5:1).

APPLICATION

John did a credible work when he developed the redemptive nature of God's love. Then with masterful skill he laid the foundation of our love as a corollary to God's loving involvement in human salvation. The concepts are parallel. *"God is love"* and He is therefore redemptive. God is redemptive and *"love is made complete among us so that we will have confidence on the day of judgment, because **in this world we are like him**"* (1 John 4:17). So we are therefore assigned redemptive involvements. Clearly, a congregation without Christ has no life (cf. 1 John 5:12). And a congregation without a mission has no heart. Just as surely as God's *"love"* had to be *"manifested"* (cf. 1 John 4:9, 10, 14), so the church also needs to show their love. Our gratitude for salvation and *"Christ's love . . . "* expressed in our behalf *"compels us . . . (to) no longer live for themselves but for him who died for them and was raised again"* (2 Corinthians 5:14-15). And that demands that we pursue the mission assignment He gave us with devotion as nearly parallel to His devotion as possible. When *"God's love is perfected in us,"* then evangelistic involvements toward *"the world"* will be natural and urgently pursued.

The First Epistle of John

Fellowship Is Rooted in the New Birth by Faith

1 John 5:1-12

Whosoever **believeth** *that Jesus is the Christ is begotten of God: and whosoever loveth him that begat loveth him also that is begotten of him* (1 John 5:1, ASV) [Emphasis added]. *Everyone who* **believes** *that Jesus is the Christ is* **born of God**, *and everyone who loves the father loves his child as well* (1 John 5:1, NIV) [Emphasis added].

The phrase *"Whosoever believeth"* (**pisteuon**) is a fuller, stronger term for faith than is used elsewhere in this epistle. As a present tense participle, this **belief** is necessary before the new birth and serves as an ongoing evidence of it. Jesus in His Great Commission ordains, *" 'Whoever believes and is baptized will be saved, but whoever does not believe will be condemned'"* (Mark 16:16). He clearly presented the privilege *"to all who received him to those who believed in his name, he gave the* **right** *to become children of God"* (John 1:12-13). Belief in the name is an essential prerequisite to *"becoming children of God"* and precedes being *"born of God."* Obviously, it is important that John be allowed to interpret John! This verse must reflect the concepts John so carefully established in his Gospel. The Hebrew writer unequivocally insists, *"And without faith it is impossible to please God, because anyone who comes to him must believe that he exists and that he rewards those who earnestly seek him"* (Hebrews 11:6). Paul also affirms, *"You are all sons of God through faith in Christ Jesus, for all of you who were baptized into Christ have clothed yourselves with Christ"* (Galatians 3:26-27). This is worthy of repetition: **whatever it takes to receive the new birth is exactly what is required to keep it intact.**

Righteousness, love, and **faith** are the **pillars** on which John erects the origin of the new birth and the post-conversion evidence of that new birth. John affirms that a commitment to a consistent practice of righteousness is a precondition to being *"born of God"* (1 John 3:9). Repentance from sin is a necessary condition for the new birth! And the practice of righteousness stands to confirm the new birth. Then as a prerequisite to being *"born of God"* John includes a settled commitment to sacrificial *"love"* (1 John 4:7). The new birth cannot occur on a platform of hate. The consistent practice of *"love"* gives evidence to the new birth. Finally, being *"born of God"* is dependent upon a prior belief *"that Jesus is the Christ."* And one's present abiding faith in Jesus is evidence of the new birth. It is futile to claim the new birth if any of those three doctrinal pillars is missing from the God-given equation developed by John.

"Jesus is the Christ" is the crucial ingredient in a believer's faith. John's concern seems to focus on the Cerinthian Gnostic claim that Jesus was not the Messiah of Old Testament prophecy. Denial of His messiahship tends to support Gnostic dualism, docetism, and many other allied errors they fostered.

The discussion of being *"born of God"* sets the stage for the origin of sacred ties to family relationships. *"Love"* for the Father of the family imposes equal *"love"* for the rest of the family. Even under the Law of Moses, according to Jesus, the *" 'most important* (commandment) *is . . . Love the Lord your God with all your heart . . . The second is this: "Love your neighbor as yourself" '"* (Mark 12:29-31).

> *Hereby we know that we love the children of God, when we love God and **do his commandments** (1 John 5:2, ASV). This is how we know that we love the children of God: by loving God and carrying out his commands (1 John 5:2, NIV).*

God's *"commandments"* are rules designed to regulate and

make noble all fraternal relations among Christians. If we believe in the loving rescue Christ accomplished for us on the cross, then genuine *"love"* for God is a logical result. And if we *"love God,"* then *"love"* for His children must become second nature for all members of God's family. Jesus insisted, *"If you love me, you will obey what I command"* (John 14:15).

To *"do his commandments"* becomes the criteria that verifies our *"love* for *the children of God."* Paul agrees, *"for he who loves his fellowman has fulfilled the law. . . (All the commandments can be) . . . summed up in this one rule* 'Love your neighbor as yourself.' Love does no harm to its neighbor. Therefore, love is the fulfillment of the law"* (Romans 13:8-10). John has already explained the full sacrificial obligation that Calvary lays upon us toward our brethren (cf. 1 John 3:16). The Cross creates a love-debt that must be paid!

> *For this is the love of God, that we keep his commandments: and his commandments are **not grievous*** (1 John 5:3, ASV) [Emphasis added]. *This is love for God: to obey his commands. And his commands are **not burdensome*** (1 John 5:3, NIV) [Emphasis added].

Our *"love of God"* (literally *"for God"*) demands that we keep on keeping His commandments. There is a logical flow in John's theology. To *"know God"* is to *"love God"*, to love Him is to love His children, and to love His children is to keep His commandments.

The phrase *"His commandments are not grievous"* (**bareiai**) assures us that God's demands are not burdensome. *"His commandments"* are not the source of human grief. It is exclusively in the violation of His commandments that all our sorrow and bitterness arise. Jesus said, *"'My yoke is easy, and my burden is light'"* (Matthew 11:30). Jesus also said that the Pharisees *"'tie up heavy (**barea**) loads and put them on men's shoulders, but they themselves are not willing to lift a finger to move them'"* (Matthew 23:4). In giving the Law of Moses, the Lord stated,

*"Now what I am commanding you today is **not** too difficult for you or beyond your reach"* (Deuteronomy 30:11). God's laws are neither too vague to comprehend nor too difficult to keep. They are not arbitrary rules designed to load His subjects with meaningless trivia.

It almost goes without saying, yet it is evident, that *"love for God"* makes the *"keeping of his commandments"* a joyful privilege and an exercise in gratitude because of redemption.

> *For **whatsoever** is begotten of God overcometh the world: and this is the victory that hath overcome the world, even our faith* (1 John 5:4, ASV) [Emphasis added]. *For **everyone** born of God overcomes the world. This is the victory that has overcome the world, even our faith* (1 John 5:4, NIV) [Emphasis added].

In 1 John 5:1 it is *"whosoever (**pas** = a personal pronoun) is begotten of God,"* but in this verse it is *"whatsoever (**pan** = a relative pronoun) is begotten of God."* Universal success is promised to everything God does or originates. Every Christian and all his God-given endowments are rooted in victory. God's *"commandments,"* His *"love,"* His revelation that engenders *"faith,"* His *"message we heard from the beginning,"* His *"witness to his Son,"* His kingdom and its ultimate victory *"at his coming"* — all these and more are victorious fruits of God's intervention into human history. These and more are the solid grounds of the Christian's victory in Christ. For **His** victories become ours through conquering *"faith."*

The word *"overcometh"* (**nika**), being a present indicative, points to a believer's **continuous victory** in the midst of their continuous struggle against *"the world."* *"Hath overcome"* (**nikasasa**), being a first aorist, may well relate to the unwavering trust Jesus Himself had in the Father that led Him to victory. He triumphantly told His disciples: *"'be of good cheer; I have overcome (**nikasesa**) the world'"* (John 16:33, ASV). Jesus was a man of faith; He both believed God and believed in God! Jesus said, *"'I will put my trust in him'"* (Hebrews 2:13). This kind of trust gave Jesus victory over *"the world."* Likewise our unwavering trust in His redemptive activity gives us victory over *"the world."* Our faith in His mission of salvation is the source of all our victories both here and now and hereafter. Indeed, *"in all things, we are more than conquerors through him who loved us"* (Romans 8:37). The victory John discusses here is further elaborated in the Revelation. Speaking of the arch-enemies of Jesus and of His people, John states:

> *'They will make war against the Lamb, but the Lamb will overcome them because he is Lord of lords and King of kings — and with him will be his called, chosen and faithful followers'* (Revelation 17:14).

> *And **who** is he that overcometh the world, but he that believeth that Jesus is the Son of God?* (1 John 5:5, ASV) [Emphasis added]. *Who is it that overcomes the world? Only he who believes that Jesus is the Son of God* (1 John 5:5, NIV).

Having digressed to the use of the relative pronoun *"whatsoever"* in 1 John 5:4, in 5:5 John returns to the personal pronoun *"whosoever."* Victorious faith is quite specific in content. The statement that *"Jesus is the Son of God"* defines his absolute deity. Belief that *"Jesus is the Christ"* is no less specific in the definition of biblical faith in His Messianic role (cf. 1 John 5:1). The *"world"* is a vanquished enemy before God's people when they have a settled conviction about the deity and messiahship of Jesus. Thus John's question is not rhetorical. Rather the question unfolds the victorious fruits of such specific faith. It is our trust in the *"blood of Jesus"* (cf. 1 John 1:7) that gives us constant *"cleansing"* from sin. This *"cleansing"* gives constant *"fellowship"* with the Father. Then our *"fellowship with the Father"* ultimately grants *"boldness"* before him in the day of judgment. To what greater victories could a Christian aspire?

> *This is he that came **by** **water and blood**, even Jesus Christ; not with the water only, but with **the water and***

with the blood (1 John 5:6a, ASV) [Emphasis added].
This is the one who came by water and blood — Jesus
Christ. He did not come by water only, but by water and
blood (1 John 5:6a, NIV) [Emphasis added].

John further expands the specifics of a Christian's faith to
include two very essential elements of Jesus' life and mission.
With the statement: *"This is he that came by,"* John introduces two
significant historical manifestations of Jesus' redemptive mission.
John's reference to *"the water and the blood"* relate to the baptism
and the crucifixion of Jesus.

Some explanation needs to be given to this context. Cerinthian
Gnosticism, historically concurrent with John's writing, promoted
an "adoptionist" view of the incarnation of Jesus. Speculations
about the person of Jesus assumed the following rationale in
Cerinthus' thinking:

Jesus was born of Joseph and Mary as a simple man,
though He was much wiser and more holy than His
peers. At His baptism by John the Baptist, Christ (the
divine Spirit) came down upon Jesus in the form of a
dove. The invading Christ suppressed the human mind of
Jesus and manipulated His life for the next three years. In
miraculous manner, that Christ inspired the heavenly
messages that Jesus imparted during his earthly tenure.
Before His crucifixion, the intrusive Christ departed from
Jesus, and allowed Him to be crucified without even
knowing why. This would be a veritable case of "body
snatching" by a "spirit-being" after His baptism, and then
the Spirit departed from Him before His crucifixion.

In answer, careful attention must be given to the prepositions
used by John in the next few verses. The instrumental case
preposition *"by"* (*dia* = through) shows the error of Cerinthian
Gnosticism. *"By"* also affirms the full deity and humanity of Jesus
before, during, and after His baptism. Then with intensified
emphasis, John uses the same *"by"* to affirm the full deity and

humanity of Jesus before, during and after His crucifixion. *"By"* defines the full divine/human nature of Jesus all the way across the two episodes Cerinthus proposed. The words: *"He came by water and blood"* are used to explain the inauguration of and glorious conclusion to Jesus' public role as the Messianic redeemer of mankind.

First John 5:5 affirms that victorious faith is built around the conviction that *"Jesus is the Son of God."* *"Jesus"* is His human name. *"Son of God"* defines His deity. Then in 1 John 5:6, John adds the *"Christ"* dimension to define His Messianic mission of redemption. That three-fold doctrine is the content of the believer's victorious faith.

The phrase *"not in the water only"* is an evident denial of a contrary opinion. John makes no concessions to alternate speculations. Some possible variation of the Cerinthian adoptionist view might concede the divine/human nature *"in the water only"* of Jesus' baptism, but would deny that deity went through the experience of the *"the blood"* in His crucifixion. Second Corinthians 5:19 affirms, with a present participle, that *"God was reconciling the world to himself in Christ"* through the death of Jesus on the cross.

And it is the Spirit that beareth witness, because the Spirit is the truth (1 John 5:6b, ASV). *And it is the Spirit who testifies, because the Spirit is truth* (1 John 5:6b, NIV).

The **third testimony** to the reality of the incarnation of Jesus Christ is *"the Spirit,"* which is quite evidently the Holy Spirit. His descent upon Jesus at His baptism, followed by the Father's avowal, *"'This is my beloved Son'"* (Matthew 4:17) stands as a witness to that reality. It was obedience to directives given by the Holy Spirit that led Jesus to *"offer himself without blemish unto God"* (Hebrews 9:14, ASV). Too, it is the Holy Spirit's inspiration of apostolic testimony that gives meaning to and explanation of Jesus' redemptive mission which was culminated at Calvary. In fact, the entire life of Jesus was lived in harmony with Spirit inspired prophecies from the Old Testament (cf. Isaiah 50:4-9) and Spirit assigned events and functions during His personal ministry (cf. Matthew 4:1; Luke 4:1, 14; 10:21). Then passages like Matthew 12:28; Acts 2:22; 10:38 show that His miracles were rooted in Holy Spirit power.

The Holy Spirit is a reliable witness, *"because the Spirit is the truth."* It must be remembered that the Holy Spirit is co-equal with the Father in deity. He then becomes the Father's witness to Jesus in 1 John 5:9-10. Apostolic testimony faithfully authenticates the record of Jesus' life, for Jesus promised them the *"Holy Spirit to guide them into all truth"* (John 16:13-15; cf. Ephesians 3:5; 1 Peter 1:12). The Holy Spirit inspired the apostolic message and the miracles He performed through them confirmed their testimony (cf. 1 Corinthians 12:4-11; 2 Corinthians 12:12; Hebrews 2:4).

Some older versions have an interpolation here that adds the words: *"in heaven, the Father, the Word and the Holy Ghost: and these three are one. And there are three that bear witness in earth."* These spurious additions were added by the Spanish heretic Priscillian who died in 385 A.D. From there it was incorporated into a Latin manuscript called Pseudo-Virgilius and some of the Latin texts containing the unauthentic section were used by the King James translators in 1611 A.D. No Greek uncial manuscript contains these words. Of the two hundred plus Greek cursive manuscripts, the words are found in only two — one from the fifteenth and the other from the sixteenth century. Clearly the words are not a part of John's original message.

> *For there are three who bear witness, the Spirit, and the water, and the blood: and the three agree in one* (1 John 5:8, ASV). *For there are three that testify: the Spirit, the water and the blood; and the three are in agreement* (1 John 5:8, NIV).

The concurring witnesses *"agree in one"* and that literally implies that they are united **into one**, so that they have one purpose and one objective — that of confirming the incarnation of God's Son, Jesus Christ. The grand design of John's affirmation is really two-fold. **First,** he wishes to contradict Gnostic error and then present the Holy Spirit to confirm the truthfulness of his testimony. **Second**, he wants to stabilize the faith of *"the children of God."* They must keep their faith in the reality of the redemptive mission the Messiah began at His baptismal consecration and then consummated in His sacrificial atonement on the cross. After all, that is the faith that keeps on overcoming the world.

> *If we receive the men, the witness of God is greater: for the witness of God is this, that he hath borne witness concerning his Son* (1 John 5:9, ASV). *We accept man's testimony, but God's testimony is greater because it is the testimony of God, which he has given about his Son* (1 John 5:9, NIV).

The witness of the Apostles presents an imposing case for belief *". . . that Jesus is the Christ, the Son of God; and that believing you may have life in his name"* (John 20:30-31). Peter insisted that they were both *"eyewitnesses"* and ear witnesses of Jesus — *"We ourselves heard this voice that came from heaven when we were with him on the sacred mountain,"* and then he proceeded to claim that God's Old Testament prophetic evidence for Jesus was *"made more certain and you will do well to pay attention to it, as to a light shining in a dark place, until the day dawns and the morning star rises in your hearts"* (2 Peter 1:16-19). John's *"little children"* had been taught by the Apostles, and they had embraced their word as being true (cf. 1 John 1:1-5; 2:21, 24; 4:6). Apostolic witness is good, but the Father's witness to Jesus *"is greater"* because God's witness is always true.

John does not go into detail about the Father's *"witness"* to Jesus unless the above reference to the *"Spirit"* is in fact one such witness. God's witness cannot be questioned! It is entirely too comprehensive, too specific, too convincing, and too imposing. The Law of Moses bore witness to the coming of Messiah (cf. Deuteronomy 18:15-19; John 5:39; Hebrews 3:5). All Old Testament prophets foretold His life and defined His mission of redemption (cf. Luke 24:26-27; 44-47; 1 Peter 1:10-12). His virgin birth (cf. Isaiah 7:14; Matthew 1:18-25; Luke 1:26-38) is a significant part of God's witness. Three times during His personal ministry the Father gave verbal witness to Jesus as recorded in Matthew 3:17, Mark 9:7, and John 12:28. Jesus' message was not His own, but was given Him by the Father (cf. John 12:49-50). Paul said that the Father *"declared him to be the Son of God with power* (miracles)*, according to the spirit of holiness* (Jesus' own divine essence) *and the resurrection from the dead"* (resurrections, being plural includes His own) (Romans 1:4, ASV). God's witness is unimpeachable and they who disbelieve it have no excuse for their unbelief (cf. Romans 1:20). Since the evidence is so strong, the Father has a right to issue His *"commandment"* that we should believe in the name of His Son Jesus Christ (cf. 1 John 3:23).

> *He that believeth on the Son of God* **hath the witness in him***: he that believeth not God hath made him a liar; because he hath not believed in the witness that God hath borne concerning his Son* (1 John 5:10, ASV) [Emphasis added]. *Anyone who believes in the Son of God has this testimony in his heart. Anyone who does not believe God has made him out to be a liar, because he has not believed the testimony God has given about his Son* (1 John 5:10, NIV).

John discusses the importance of receiving *"the witness"* the Father has given concerning His Son. To receive *"the witness"* is equivalent to believing on the Son. God's *"witness"* is external to the believer, but when faith grows out of the Father's testimony, then the *"witness"* becomes internal. The *"witness"* takes root in the heart of the believer because the evidence from God generates unwavering faith in Jesus.

The statement *"hath the witness in him"* affirms that God's *"witness"* given to Jesus is also given to all who *"are sons of God through faith in Christ Jesus"* (Galatians 3:26). God gave His testimony — His *"witness"* that Jesus is His Son. So when an obedient believer receives God's *"witness,"* then God bears *"witness"* to the believer's "sonship." Paul insists, *"The Spirit* *himself **beareth witness** with our spirit, that we are children of God"* (Romans 8:16, ASV). Paul proceeds to conclude that divine sonship issues into divine inheritance (cf. Romans 8:17). So does John in 1 John 5:11, for God's *"witness"* about the believer issues into *"eternal life."*

The phrase *"Anyone who does not believe God"* not only rejects God's testimony about Jesus, but *"has made him out to be a liar."* There are two perfect tense verbs here that define a permanent condition that disbelief produces. The unbeliever makes God a permanent *"liar,"* because he is a permanent disbeliever in the witness God continues to give Jesus in His word.

> *And the witness is this, that God gave unto us eternal life, and this life is in his Son* (1 John 5:11, ASV). *And this is the testimony: God has given us eternal life, and this life is in his Son* (1 John 5:11, NIV).

Beyond the content of God's *"witness"* about Jesus and about the children of God, there is the quality of *"life"* Christians enjoy as a consequence of being in Christ. John insists that *"eternal life"* is intrinsically bound up in Jesus. God's witness is again two-fold:
1) *"God has given* (aorist tense) *us eternal life."*
2) *"This life is in his Son."*

The obvious impact of John's statement is that Christians **now** possess *"eternal life."* The term *"eternal"* relates to the quality of the life and not its duration. The *"life"* John discusses here is centered in Christ and confirmed in John 1:4, *"In him was life, and that life was the light of men."* Keep in mind that this verse says "God gave us eternal life." It does not say "God eternally gave us life!"

> *He that hath the Son hath the life; he that hath not the Son of God hath not the life* (1John 5:12, ASV). *He who has the Son has life; he who does not have the Son of God does not have life* (1 John 5:12, NIV).

The phrase *"hath* (present participle) *the life"* defines the *"eternal life"* of verse 11 as a <u>present possession</u>. A present possession does not equate automatically into a <u>forever possession</u>. Remember that the word *"eternal"* is an adjective of **quality** rather than an adverb of quantity or duration. It would be no more proper to affirm from this verse (as some do) that the one who has the Son <u>eternally</u> has Him, than it would be proper to affirm that the one who does not have the Son <u>eternally</u> does not have Him! Great confusion is generated when adjectives of **quality** are erroneously turned into adverbs of quantity! John will make it clear in the next few verses that a man who presently *"has eternal life"* can definitely lose that life by committing a *"sin unto death."*

APPLICATION

Biblical faith has specific elements that are basic to the reception of the new birth. Those specifics are equally basic to the continuance of that new life. Salvation begins when one confesses his conviction that the man Jesus is the divine Son of God and on that faith is baptized for the remission of his sins (cf. Acts 2:38; 8:36-37; Romans 10:9-10). The new birth has obligations that are equally basic to its practice. Love for God and His family must manifest itself in continual obedience to God's commands, especially as they dictate duties toward his children. Present and eternal victories are intrinsically bound up in world conquering faith. Christ is the key to *"life"* both here and hereafter.

The Assurance of Life

1 John 5:13-17

These things have I written unto you, that ye may know that ye have eternal life, even unto you that believe on the name of the Son of God (1 John 5:13, ASV). *I write these things to you who believe in the name of the Son of God so that you may know that you have eternal life* (1 John 5:13, NIV).

There are two Greek words that are translated **"know."** *Ginosko* is the general term for learning. *Oida* is a deeper kind of knowledge which represents the finished learning process. *Oida* comes about when God's revelation becomes a settled conviction. *Oida* is based on God's *"witness"* to His Son and is verified by apostolic testimony in what they heard, saw, beheld, handled, and then *"declared unto us"* (1 John 1:1-4). John uses the deeper kind of knowledge (*oida*) in 1 John 5:15 (twice) and again in 1 John 5: 18-20.

The phrase *"even unto you that believe"* is a simple reaffirmation of the fact that our faith is the victory that leads to *"life."* To *"believe on the name of the Son of God"* is to accept all the things His name signals about His deity and His redemptive mission.

> *And this is the boldness which we have toward him, that, if we ask anything according to his will, he heareth us* (1 John 5:14, ASV). *This is the confidence we have in approaching God: that if we ask anything according to his will, he hears us* (1 John 5:14, NIV).

The Christian's prayer life is enhanced by the knowledge that he **now** *"has eternal life."* Not only is he *"bold"* (**parresia**) in asking anything, he is also confident of God's certain answer. John's *"whatsoever"* in 1 John 3:22 and *"anything"* here challenges our thinking about the unlimited content of our prayers to God.

The phrase *"according to his will"* does not diminish the *"anything"* that may be included in our prayers. Nor does it imply that we must second-guess God and only ask for those things He wants for us. Nor does it mean that we are authorized to pray only for those things the Bible authorizes by word or implication. *"According to his will"* is an adverbial phrase that relates to the asking and does not limit the *"anything"* we may ask for. It defines the **attitude** with which we ask. There is deep trust in God's *"will"* for our lives expressed in the phrase. We are encouraged to ask God to grant our request *"according to **his** will"* and **not ours**!

This kind of attitude protects us from selfish ambitions and personal greed. Even Jesus confronted some of His most urgent feelings and desires experienced in the Garden of Gethsemane with the surrender of His own will. If we can learn to be comfortable with God's *"will"* in our lives, then our prayers will be filled with greater boldness and God's answers to us will be more responsive and helpful.

If we ask for something we believe would bless our lives, and ask it *"according to his will,"* if He grants it, we should say, "Thank you, Lord." If we ask for it, and He does not grant it, we should still say, "Thank you, Lord." We asked that His will be done, and it was done; we should be equally grateful in either case. With such an attitude, we may be assured that every prayer will be answered. Thus the higher will of God is realized in our lives, as we are blessed for wanting only what God wants for us. ***"He hears us"*** is an affirmation that our prayers are both heard by God and are answered by God. (cf. 1 Peter 3:10-12).

> And ***if*** *we know that he heareth us whatsoever we ask, we know that we have the petitions which we have asked of him* (1 John 5:15, ASV) [Emphasis added]. *And* ***if*** *we know that he hears us — whatever we ask — we know that we have what we asked of him* (1 John 5:15, NIV).

John's ***"if"*** (a subordinate conjunction) assumes as true that God does *"hear"* our prayers. As surely as we *"know"* (***oidamen***) that God *"hears"* us, it is just that sure that we *"know"* (***oidamen***) that we have the requests we make of Him. Remember that **he who asks** is the one that **receives**. Remembering this fact will help us to understand the next two verses.

> *If any man see his brother sinning a sin not unto death, he shall ask, and God will give him life for them that sin not unto death. There is a sin unto death: not concerning this do I say that he should make requests* (1 John 5:16, ASV). *If anyone see his brother commit a sin that does not lead to death, he should pray and God will give him*

life. I refer to those whose sin does not lead to death.
There is a sin that leads to death. I am not saying that he
should pray about that (1 John 5:16, NIV).

John is still discussing prayer as indicated by the phrase *"he shall ask"* and *"he should not make requests."* Apparently he is presenting a critical example of prayers *"according to God's will"* and those that are not. At this point it would be easy to digress from John's prayer topic and focus on the *"sin unto"* or *"not unto death,"* but that would cause us to lose the explanation John offers about the awesome power of intercessory prayer.

Without controversy the greatest gift that could be obtained through prayer for a troubled brother would be the gift of *"life."* It goes without saying that if the greatest gift could be gained through prayer, then surely no lessor gift would be denied.

John is discussing the prayer of a Christian who is concerned about a fellow Christian. When any *"brother"* is *"sinning a sin"* his spiritual survival is in jeopardy. Alarm is automatically triggered in other Christians who *"love the children of God"* (1 John 5: 2-3). Rather than gossip to others about the struggling brother, the first step *"love"* demands is intercession before God on his behalf. The prayer is *"bold"* — it requests *"life"* for the brother! The *"life"* sought is evidently spiritual. John wants the *"brother"* who prays to *"know"* (**oidamen**) that God indeed does hear his prayer and that he has the answer which he has asked of Him. He prays knowing that *"God will give him life"* for those whose sin *"is not unto death."*

Since the first sentence of this verse contains two nouns and five pronouns, it can be helpful in understanding John's statement to give proper names in all seven cases. With assigned names inserted the sentence would read: *"If anyone* (we will call this anyone Sam) *sees his* (Sam's) *brother* (we will call the brother Pete) *sinning a sin not unto death, he* (Sam) *shall ask, and he* (God) *will give him* (Sam) *life for them* (the life is for Pete and others like him) *that sin not unto death."* It is Sam who offered the prayer, and it is Sam who receives God's answer! The New American Standard Version properly translates this verse, *"he shall ask and God will for him give life to them."* Pete did not even pray (not in this verse). However, Pete does receive *"life"* from God because of Sam's intercession. But it is Sam who receives the answer to his prayer! God is pleased with Sam's concern for Pete's spiritual survival. He honors Sam's prayer by granting his request. Jesus' parable of the vine-dresser is **not** a parallel to John's example. Yet I like to think that the Lord of the vineyard granted the petition of his vine-dresser who asked for a year's extension of life to the barren fig tree (cf. Luke 13:6-9). At least in John's example, the Lord is favorably inclined toward the prayer of another "vine-dresser" of sorts. It is easy to suppose that Sam's first action after his prayer would be a visit to Pete to inform him of his concern.

As yet Pete's sin is *"not unto death."* So he still has *"life,"* though his sin places his fellowship with God in peril. The sin is *"not unto death"* so the *"life"* God *"gives"* must be an extension of that *"life."* It might be that Pete is struggling with a long habit of sin and is about ready to give up trying to be a Christian. It may be that God, as the Lord of the vineyard, may be on the verge of giving up on Pete because of his sin problems. In either case, John assures his readers that boldness in prayer is heard, answered, and appreciated by God. It would be easy to verbalize Sam's prayer and sense his loving concern. Obviously Pete needs to repent, but that is not the point of John's discussion!

The phrase *"a sin not unto death"* clearly reaffirms John's message in 1 John 1:7 and 9. The Christian who is *"walking in the light"* is therefore walking under the blood of Jesus and his sins do not break his fellowship with God. His sins are *"not unto death."* If he becomes presumptuous and ceases to *"walk in the light,"* then he loses the constant cleansing that Jesus' blood offers. His sins are *"unto death"* (cf. Ezekiel 33:13,18). In such cases, John simply does not encourage prayer though He does not prohibit it. Since *"there is no darkness"* in God (1 John 1:5) it is not proper to ask God to give *"life"* to one who is *"walking"* in darkness. God will not give *"life"* to a prodigal son who is still living in the pig pen. Jeremiah was prohibited to pray for impenitent Israel (cf. Jeremiah 7:16; 11:14; 14:11-12).

The words *"unto"* and *"not unto"* are directional prepositions that define the course or orientation one has when the sin is committed. The *"sin unto death"* (**harmatia pros thanaton**) is committed when one turns away from light, life, God, and walks in *"darkness"* and *"death."* A *"sin not unto death"* (**me pros thanaton**) is committed when one is facing *"life,"* while *"walking in the light"* toward God.

In the context of John's epistle the specific sin could be the practice of Gnostic antinomian immorality or it might be following the heretical teachings of *"antichrist."* It could be one's denial of faith in Christ because of persecution. In any case, it is not the *"blasphemy of the Holy Spirit"* of Matthew 12:31-32 (ASV) as many commentaries assume. The man Jesus discussed in the Matthew context never became a Christian and his *"blasphemy shall not be forgiven him, neither in this world* (age of the Mosaic dispensation) *nor in that which is to come"* (the Christian dispensation). John is definitely discussing a Christian *"brother."* In fact a Christian is the only person who can commit *"a sin unto death,"* because a Christian is the only one who has *"life"* that can be destroyed by sin. There are no suicides among the dead! John is dealing with a Christian who commits spiritual suicide.

John's statement *"If any man sees"* assures his readers that they can generally distinguish between those whose sins are *"not unto death"* from those whose sins are *"unto death."* It is easy to *"see"* a person's attitude toward his sin, his humility when discussing it, his evident struggle against it, and his frequent prayers for strength to resist it. All this shows something of the direction he is facing in his efforts to live the Christian life. But when a person becomes belligerent about his sin, refuses admonition from others, and rejects correction, his direction is easily detected!

John says, *"There is sin unto death,"* but it is not necessarily irreversible. Though John does not encourage prayer requests in such cases, from other Scripture it is evident that concerned brethren can and should intervene when a *"brother is overtaken in any trespass"* and therefore needs *"to be restored"* (Galatians 6:1, ASV). Paul told Timothy that Christians must *"gently instruct"* those who oppose them:

> And the Lord's servant must not quarrel; instead, he
> must be kind to everyone, able to teach, not resentful.
> Those who oppose him he must gently instruct, in the
> hope that God will grant them repentance leading them
> to a knowledge of the truth and that they will come to
> their senses and escape from the trap of the devil, who
> has taken them captive to do his will (2 Timothy 2:24-
> 26).

Repentance and restoration to *"life"* is available to any erring
"brother." James is very emphatic when he says:

> My brothers, if one of you should wander from the truth
> and someone should bring him back, remember this:
> Whoever turns a sinner from the error of his way will
> save him from death and cover over a multitude of sins
> (James 5:19-20).

In the parable of the Prodigal Son the Father told the older
brother, *"'My son . . . you are always with me . . . this brother of
yours was dead and is alive again; he was lost and is found'"*
(Luke 15:32). His sin had been *"a sin unto death,"* but he was
restored to *"life."*

> All unrighteousness is sin: and there is a sin not unto
> death (1 John 5:17, ASV). All wrongdoing is sin, and
> there is sin that does not lead to death (1 John 5:17,
> NIV).

The **second** general definition John gives for sin is
"unrighteousness" (**adikia**) — the opposite of *"righteous"*
(**dikaion**). Sin is also *"lawlessness"* (**anomia**) (1 John 3:4). Clearly
John is not suggesting categories of sins that are fatal and others
that are not. Any specific sin could be *"unto death."* For one
Christian, a sin may be *"not unto death"* while the same sin might

be *"unto death"* for another Christian. There are a number of factors that might determine the consequence of any sin. The spiritual maturity of the one sinning, the haughtiness with which it is committed, the doctrinal perversions it represents, and the menace it may bring to the rest of the church — all these might enter the equation. For John sin is sin and potentially fatal to the soul. Though he insists that not all *"sin is unto death,"* ultimately, the question of sin being fatal or not is determined by whether or not the *"blood of Jesus"* is allowed by God to *"cleanse"* it.

Clearly Roman Catholics who attempt to sustain their concepts of "mortal and venial sins" are as foreign to John's doctrine as was the antinomian gnosticism of his day.

APPLICATION

It is not an empty boast to claim the present possession of eternal life in Christ. It is based on revealed truth. Some feel that such a claim will cause brethren to believe they cannot be lost. John did not share such fears. There may be a contrary fear that would cause some to believe they cannot be saved! John certainly would discourage such a perversion of his teaching. Remember that this epistle of John's develops the theology of assurance.

The section just studied encourages sober concern for struggling brethren. It is clear that John wants *"love for the brethren"* to be real, practical, prayerful, and involved. The ultimate survival and salvation of the souls may depend upon timely prayerful intervention for *"one another."* One has to be impressed with the concessions God makes to intercessory prayers offered for weak brethren! And yet is seems that so few manifest the deep concern for a straying brother discussed in this context. The *"one another"* assignments found in the New Testament imperatively impose all that the above verses demand and much more!

Fellowship is Rooted
In Jesus' Present Ministry

1 John 5:18-21

*We know that whosoever **is begotten** of God sinneth not; but **he** that was begotten of God keepeth himself, and the evil one toucheth him not* (1 John 5:18, ASV) [Emphasis added]. *We know that anyone born of God does not continue to sin; the one who was born of God keeps him safe, and the evil one cannot harm him* (1 John 5:18, NIV).

John concludes this epistle with a restatement of three basic things God's children *"know"* (**oidamen**) by divine revelation. We *"know"* that we are protected by Christ (cf. 1 John 5:18). We *"know"* that we are God's children, and that the world is lost (cf. 1 John 5:19). We *"know"* that Jesus came and He *"has given us understanding"* (cf. 1 John 5:20).

The discussion about *"sins unto"* or *"not unto death"* gives rise to John's renewed insistence that a believer with a standing new birth does not practice habitual, death-dealing sin. The phrase *"is begotten"* is a perfect tense verb that defines the regenerate man whose new birth is still intact. He *"sinneth not"* (present indicative) and that is the reason his new birth stands. John already established that *"he that doeth righteousness is begotten of God"* (cf. 1 John 2:29; 3:9).

*"**He** that was begotten"* (aorist participle) probably relates to Christ who is the protector and "keeper" of God's children. Christ assures God's children that *"'no one can snatch them out of my hand'"* (John 10:28). Clearly it is the Christ who Jude is talking about when he wrote, *"To him who is able to keep you from falling and to present you before his glorious presence without fault and with great joy"* (Jude 24). The Christian is protected by his Master. *"The evil one"* is Satan. He cannot ravage the flock of the Good Shepherd. Such an assertion must not be taken to imply that it is impossible to be a *"lost sheep"* or a *"lost son"* as Jesus clearly

taught in Luke 15.

*We know that we are of God, and the whole world **lieth** in the evil one* (1 John 5:19, ASV) [Emphasis added]. *We know that we are children of God, and that the whole world **is under the control** of the evil one* (1 John 5:19, NIV) [Emphasis added].

The words *"of God"* (**ek** = out of God) trace our spiritual roots to His saving grace through Christ. Such a bold statement grows out of John's affirmation that we *"know that we have eternal life."* The assurance given here offers great consolation from an apostolic source. It certainly invalidates the Gnostic denial that John's *"little children"* are genuine Christians.

John says, *"the whole world"* which consists of the unbelieving and unregenerate **"lie"** (**keitai** = as one dead, cf. Matthew 28:6) in the grasp of the *"evil one"* (**pornero** = wicked). Throughout this epistle John has drawn sharp lines of separation between the *"children of God"* and the *"children of the devil"* (1 John 3:10). The dividing line is defined by *"the spirit of truth"* versus *"the spirit of falsehood"* (1 John 4:6). It manifests the settled practice of *"walking in light"* and *"love"* or of *"walking in darkness"* and *"hate"* (cf. 1 John 1:6-7; 2:8-11).

Surely the glories that spring from being *"of God"* contrasted with the pathetic destiny of those *"in the evil one"* should stir urgent evangelistic involvements of the those who are *"of God"* toward those who are *"in the evil one."*

*And we know that the Son of God **is come**, and hath given us an understanding, that we know him that is true, and we are in him that is true, even in his Son Jesus Christ. This is true God and eternal life* (1 John 5:20, ASV) [Emphasis added]. *We know also that the Son of God has come and has given us understanding, so that we may know him who is true. And we are in him who is true — even in his Son Jesus Christ. He is the true God and eternal life* (1 John 5:20, NIV).

The phrase *"is come"* is a perfect tense verb that defines the abiding result of the incarnation of Jesus. The fact is, perhaps incidental to John's thought, that Jesus is **still** *"the son of man"* (cf. John 5:27; Acts 17:31; 1 Timothy 2:5). Jesus promised to remain with His people (cf. Matthew 28:20). The *"understanding"* (*dianoian* = perception) He brought to our intelligence gives us the ability to *"know"* (*ginosko*) through education and to *"know"* (*oida*) through revelation both God and Christ fully. The *"understanding"* seems to be another synonym for John's earlier term, which he called *"the anointing"* (cf. 1 John 2:20, 27). This *"understanding"* acquaints us with Jesus who *"is true."* He is real, an apostolic reality which is contrasted with the *docetic* (only seemed to be) speculations of the Gnostics. The *"understanding"* not only reveals Jesus Christ to us, it gives us *"knowledge"* of how we may be saved through an obedient faith in Him. To be *"in him"* is to share in His life and *"abide in him and he in us"* (1 John 3:24, ASV).

The phrase *"this is true God"* clearly means *"this one"* is divine. John is making his strongest affirmation of the absolute deity of Jesus Christ. Real deity is affirmed here perhaps to expose the false and misleading idolatries of theological error in 1 John 5:21.

The phrase *"and eternal life"* shows how John equates salvation with faith in the divinity of Jesus Christ. If he is not *"true God,"* then *"eternal life"* through Him is an illusion (cf. John 17:7).

> *My little children, guard yourselves from idols* (1 John 5:21, ASV). *Dear children, keep yourselves from idols* (1 John 5:21).

Gnostics have created their own theologies and even invented the gods that go with their speculations. Their god is not concerned about morality. He is not affected by sin. He is really a product of human speculation and is not a God at all. He is just an unreal figment of man's imagination. John, therefore, properly warns his readers to be on guard against such man-made *"idols."*

APPLICATION

The Christian has confident assurance of his salvation in Christ Jesus. The redemptive mission of Messiah has the backing of the *"witness of God,"* the truths announced by the Apostles, and the Christian's own *"knowledge"* that has grown out of all the sources of divine revelation. Any denial of the foundations of our faith jeopardizes all hope of ultimate salvation through Christ. Anything less than the confession of the human/divine person of Messiah is another form of idolatry.

The Second Epistle of John

INTRODUCTION

The epistles of <u>Second</u> and <u>Third John</u> continue the general theme presented in First John. There John's primary purpose was to affirm apostolic testimony about Jesus' person and message. A secondary purpose was to expose the theological, moral, and social errors gnostic teachers of his day tried to introduce into Christian doctrine. In 1 John 4:1-6 the author imperatively commanded his readers to *"believe not every spirit,"* but with an equally imperative command insisted that they *"prove the spirits, whether they are of God."* The presence of *"many false prophets . . . are gone out into the world"* justifies the order to *"prove"* them. In that context John gave the criteria by which the *"proving"* should be made. Clearly some teachers are *"of God,"* and they teach the message received from the Apostles. Others are not *"of God"* and deny the apostolic testimony. The *"of God"* and *"not of God"* defines the difference between *"the spirit of truth"* that motivated God's acknowledged spokesmen and *"the spirit of error"* that characterized gnostic teachers.

In his first epistle John established the identity of the above mentioned teachers and the doctrines they espoused. He was cautious to warn believers about the spiritual dangers involved in giving heed to those *"false prophets."* Their ultimate salvation was at stake! John opportunely identified the respective sources of information upon which each class of teacher relied. *"We are of God,"* John claimed for the Apostles. Therefore, God was the prime source of their message. *"They are of the world"* and they speak from the viewpoint of the world, John says of the Gnostics. That is their epistemology. Their so-called knowledge came from subjective human speculations.

First John addresses collectively those John calls *"my little children."* His concern is that they protect themselves from gnostic encroachments through the errors they fostered. In <u>Second John</u> the Apostle is careful to inform the believers how they should deal with false teachers. They must not give them an audience nor assist them in the spread of their error (cf. 2 John 7-10). In <u>Third John</u> the Apostle is equally careful to instruct the believers what their response must be to those who are missionaries of the truth. They must offer them hospitality when they come and support them when they go forth on their mission.

The Practice of Christian Hospitality

In New Testament times Christians traveling away from home were dependent on their brethren for hospitality. This was particularly true of missionaries. This would especially apply to the Twelve and the Seventy when Jesus sent them out announcing the Kingdom. He said, *"'Whatever town or village you enter, search for some worthy person there and stay at his house until you leave'"* (Matthew 10:11). As they entered a *"worthy"* house, they were to *"'stay in that house, eating and drinking whatever they give you'"* (Luke 10:7). Hebrews 13:2 commanded Christians, *"Do not forget to entertain strangers, for by so doing some people have entertained angels without knowing it."* Lydia apparently insisted that a reluctant Paul and company accept hospitality in her home. She wanted to have a part in the glorious ministry of spreading the Gospel. Luke said, *"She begged us, saying, 'If you have judged me to be faithful to the Lord, come to my house, and abide there.' And she <u>constrained us</u>"* (Acts 16:15, ASV). When Paul wrote to the Romans from Corinth, he sent salutations from *"Gaius, whose hospitality I and the whole church here enjoy"* (Romans 15:23). In Caesarea and in Ptolemais, Paul's company stayed in homes of the brethren (cf. Acts 21:7-8). Later, Paul and his entourage stayed in the home of Mnason of Cyrpus (cf. Acts 18:16).

There were no motels available in New Testament times. The

available inns for travelers were generally houses of ill-repute. William Barclay notes, "Inns were notoriously dirty and flea-infested, while 'inn keepers' were notoriously rapacious." Thus it was very important for Christians to offer lodging for traveling brethren. Gospel preachers and missionaries were particularly dependent upon such a practice. Of course, there were false teachers who tried to avail themselves of the same privilege. Therefore, John urged them not to give their hospitality to heretics, but Christians did have an obligation toward those who proclaimed the apostolic message.

Truths Reaffirmed, Warnings Issued

John used his second epistle to reaffirm some of the major theological, moral, and social obligations more extensively affirmed in First John. He is particularly intent on stabilizing the believers faith in the truth about Christ and on their consistent practice of *"righteousness"* and fraternal *"love."* Apostolic truth lives in Christians and it will abide there forever (cf. 2 John 2). *"Righteousness"* is the product of walking after his commandments (cf. 2 John 6). The *"love"* assignment derives from the *"new commandment"* which we had from the beginning (cf. 2 John 5).

Who Is *"The Elder"*?

John identifies himself with the title *"the elder."* The term *"elder"* (*`O presbuteros* = an older man) probably does not indicate a position in a local congregational eldership. Peter appealed as a "fellow elder" among other elders (cf. 1 Peter 5:1), but John seems to refer to his advanced years — as an old man. John presents himself as one of the original twelve who received their message directly from the Father (cf. 2 John 4) and the commandment of love which he received from Christ (cf. 2 John 5). Thus he distinguishes the *"we"* (Apostles) from the *"you"* (apostolic disciples) in verses 4-8. He felt obliged to discuss *"many* *things"* with his readers, which he preferred to deal with personally rather than *"with paper and ink"* (2 John 12; cf. 3 John 13). Such language has an apostolic ring to it. This is especially true in his denunciation of Diotrephes, *"So if I come, I will call attention to what he is doing, gossiping maliciously about us* (the Apostles) (3 John 10). The language here seems parallel to Paul's apostolic warning given in 2 Corinthians 13:10.

Who Is the *"Elect Lady?*

The debate over the identity of the *"elect lady"* revolves around two different views among commentaries. The first seems more plausible and has several valid arguments to support it. Accordingly, the *"elect lady"* would be the personification of a congregation of Christians well known to John. The *"lady"* would be a church, and *"her children"* would be individual members. As the *"bride of Christ"* (cf. Ephesians 5:22-33; 2 Corinthians 11:2; Revelation 21:9), the church naturally takes on the name of her Lord (Greek = **Kurios**). Thus His royalty is by relationship conferred upon her as His *"lady"* (**Kuria**), as His bride. The church is divinely *"elected"* (**eklekte**) to share in Christ's regal dignity. Peter, in his letter to the *"elect (**syneklete**) who are sojourners of the Dispersion"* (1 Peter 1:1, ASV), will later send greetings from their fellow Christians: *"She that is in Babylon, elect together (**syneklekte**) with you, saluteth you"* (1 Peter 5:13, ASV). The title of a "Royal Lady" (the counter-part of a "Royal Lord") would be a very appropriate title for the .church.

The second and less plausible opinion would make the *"elect lady"* a Christian woman who belonged to some established Grecian aristocracy. Accordingly, her family name would be *"Kyria, "* and her given name *"Eklekte. "* Some of the principle arguments that militate against this view are found in the text of 2 John. It would not be probable that this *"Eklekte Kyria"* would have a sister with the same name — *"The children of thine elect sister (**Adelphes son tes eklektes**) salute thee"* (2 John 13, ASV). Those *"children"* more appropriately refers to members of a sister congregation of believers.

Again John would not likely mention his *"love"* for her and *"her children"* as a *"command which we had from the beginning"* (2 John 5, ASV). John frequently switches from the second person singular *"whom"* (vs. 1) and *"ye"* (vs. 4 and 5) to the second person plural *"ye"* (vs. 6), *"yourselves"* (vs. 8), *"you"* (vs. 10, 12), and then finally back to the second person singular *"thine"* (vs. 13). Such shifting between singular and plural pronouns seems to indicate that John is addressing a community of believers rather than an individual. In Third John the noun *"Gaius"* and all pronouns directed to him are consistently second person singulars! John R. W. Stott remarks: "John's language is not appropriate to a real person, either in his statement of love (1-2) or in his exhortation to love (5). The elder could hardly refer to his personal love for a lady and her children as a 'command' which 'we have had from the beginning.'" In the final analysis the question of the identity of the *"Elect Lady"* is probably more a question of academic interest than of practical importance.

Some commentaries have suggested that Second John was written from Ephesus. There is little information available from which to affirm or deny the claim. It is probably true that John's statement *"I wrote somewhat unto the church"* (3 John 9) is really talking about his second epistle to the *"Elect Lady."* If that is true, then the identity of the *"Elect Lady"* (2 John 1) is none other than *"the church"* to whom he wrote (3 John 9). Now to the verse by verse study of 2 John.

Reaffirmation of Truths Already Taught

2 John 1-3

The elder unto the elect lady and her children, whom I love in truth; and not I only, but also all they that know the truth (1 John 1, ASV). *The elder, to the chosen lady and her children, whom I love in the truth — and not I only, but also all who know the truth* (2 John 1, NIV).

"The elder," as John refers to himself, probably indicates his advanced age rather than a position in a local congregational eldership. Such a title adds dignity to his message. His love and concern for his *"little children"* has not decreased through the years. Nor has his faith in Christ diminished. Nor yet has his open opposition to gnostic heresies abated. Though John introduces himself in the third person, *"The elder,"* he immediately changes to the first person *"I,"* which is quite characteristic of Greek writers.

The phrase *"unto the elect lady and her children"* identifies the recipients of this brief letter. As suggested in the introduction, John is probably addressing a congregation of Christians who are faithfully holding to the truth he had already communicated to them. The Apostle hastens to reaffirm his affection for them *"whom I love in truth."* His *"in truth"* speaks of the great capacity of his devotion. It is not a casual connection John establishes between *"love"* and *"truth."* It is the *"truth"* that motivates John's affirmation of *"love"* for the *"elect lady and her children."* The *"truth"* of *"God's love for us"* imposes a *"love"* debt toward all God's family. John says, *"Dear friends, since God so loved us, we also ought to love one another"* (1 John 4:11, cf. 4:20, 21; 5:1).

The phrase *"not only I, but also all they that know the truth"* shows a common fraternal esteem for the brotherhood. Such mutual *"love"* is enjoined upon all believers toward all fellow Christians. John is not the only Apostle to impose inter-congregational *"love."* The Apostle Peter imperatively commanded *"love the brotherhood"* (1 Peter 2:17). It is interesting to notice the verb tense John used in his inclusion of *"all **they** that **know** the truth."* *"They know,"* as a perfect tense verb, says that they have come to *"know the truth,"* and they **still** *"know"* it.

For the truth's sake which abideth in us, and it shall be with us for ever (2 John 2, ASV). *Because of the truth, which lives in us and will be with us forever* (2 John 2, NIV).

Apostolic *"truth"* was intended to be a permanent guide for a believer's life. It was not subject to evolution or a new edition. Peter said, *"The word of God abideth forever"* (1 Peter 1:23-25). John's statement about the *"truth . . . which abideth"* (present indicative) insists that the *"truth"* was not only understood by them but was also a welcomed resident or guest in their heart. Jesus' statement *"if you abide in my word"* becomes a precondition to being His *"disciple"* (John 8:31).

The phrase *"it shall be with us forever"* is a confident affirmation about the *"forever"* presence of the *"truth"* that stabilizes the believer's convictions. Gnostics departed from the apostolic message, but that message will forever remain unchanged. This *"truth"* must never be compromised for any reason. Such an emphatic declaration about the eternal nature of God's *"truth"* assures believers both then and now that the Holy Scriptures forever remain his unique guide in doctrine and practice in all religious matters. Jesus was unequivocal in His affirmation that *"my words; that very word which I spoke will condemn him at the last day"* (John 12:48). Jesus' words will judge all men on that final day.

> *Grace, mercy, peace shall be with us, from God the Father, and from Jesus Christ, the Son of the Father, in truth and love* (2 John 3, ASV). *Grace, mercy and peace from God the Father and from Jesus Christ, the Father's Son, will be with us in truth and love* (2 John 3, NIV).

The words *"Grace, mercy, and peace"* contain a triad of God's gifts that form the typical apostolic salutation to the churches. It may seem trite to repeat here the general definitions given each of these qualities of God's benevolence toward His children. It is nevertheless worthy of consideration. **"Grace"** is classically defined as God's <u>unmerited favor</u> toward the <u>undeserving</u>. *"Grace"* always freely supplies that which cannot be earned. **"Mercy,"** when it is granted, spares the recipient from the punishment he <u>does deserve</u>. When God's *"grace"* offers us heaven, which we <u>do not deserve</u>, and His *"mercy"* saves us from hell, which we <u>do deserve</u>, then we have *"peace"* with God. ***"Peace"*** not only signals the cessation of all hostility, it introduces an atmosphere of positive good will between the parties involved.

"From God the Father and from Jesus Christ" defines the heavenly arena from which those three qualities flow. *"Jesus Christ"* is presented as *"the Son of the Father,"* insisting on the absolute deity of *"the Son."* The dative mood of *"in love and truth"* implies that *"love and truth"* are as much gifts from God as are the *"grace, mercy and peace."*

"The Truth Will Be With Us Forever"

2 John 4-13

*I rejoice greatly that I have found **certain** of thy children walking in truth, even as we received commandment from the Father* (2 John 4, ASV) [Emphasis added]. *It has given me great joy to find **some** of your children walking in the truth, just as the Father commanded us* (2 John 4, NIV) [Emphasis added].

The word "certain" in this verse is italicized in manuscripts, indicating that it is not really a part of the text. It is rather a loose translation of the Greek word ***ek***. ***Ek*** in Greek generally means out of or from. John does not seem to imply that some of those *"children"* are *"walking in truth"* while others among them are not. It may be that some have been influenced by gnostic errors, which would severely displease the Apostle. Apparently some of those Christians had recently visited with John, and he was delighted in their fidelity to the *"truth"* of God. In his first letter, John had complimented the brethren because *"the word of God abides in you"* (1 John 2:14, ASV). He assured them of his confidence in them because *"you know the truth"* (1 John 2:21).

"Walking (present active participle) *in truth"* defines a settled, consistent life-style directed by God's *"truth."* The Apostle says

he has *"no greater joy"* than *"to hear of my children walking in the truth"* (3 John 4). Such apostolic delight in the fidelity of their converts explains Paul's exclamation to the brethren:

> *For what is our hope, our joy, or the crown in which we will glory in the presence of our Lord Jesus when he comes? Is it not you? Indeed, you are our glory and joy* (1 Thessalonians 2:19-20).

In this epistle there are things that cheer the Apostle. There are things that disturb him about which he will give emphatic warnings. His first interest is to rejoice in the loyalty of his *"little children"* to the *"truth"* he had taught them. And he is delighted that their devotion to that *"truth"* issued into a career of practicing it.

> *And now I beseech thee, lady, not as though I wrote to thee a new commandment, but that which we had from the beginning, that we love one another* (2 John 5, ASV). *And now, dear lady, I am not writing you a new command but one we have had from the beginning. I ask that we love one another* (2 John 5, NIV).

The phrase *"I beseech thee"* (**erotao** = to ask or entreat) issues almost as a prayer from John. He is urging his readers never to neglect their assignment to *"love."* His *"no new commandment"* is indeed the original *"new commandment"* of Jesus in John 13:34 (See notes on 1 John 2:7-8). *"That which we had from the beginning"* probably goes back to their earliest enlightenment about the demands of *"love"* as contained in Jesus' *"new commandment."*

> *And this is love, that we should walk after his commandments. This is the commandment, even as ye heard from the beginning, that ye should walk in it* (2 John 6, ASV). *And this is love: that we walk in obedience*

to his commands. As you have heard from the beginning, his command is that you walk in love (2 John 5, NIV).

The phrase *"this is love"* confirms what Jesus taught: *"If you love me, you will keep my **commandments**"* (John 14:15). Both Jesus and John insist on the plurality of the *"**commandments**"* of Jesus, thus embracing all of them and practicing all of them! Our *"love for him"* is the motivational spring-board from which commandment keeping derives. Therefore, John explains with causal connection how *"love"* issues into keeping faith with our assignments.

John says, *"And this is love, **that** (**hina** = in order that) we should walk after his commandments"* — without *"love"* commandment keeping is impossible. The *"walk"* is a present active subjunctive. It defines **consistency** and **constancy** of purpose. John's discussion here about *"walking **after** (**kata** = according to) his commandments"* gives rise to his discussion in the next few verses about *"the anti-christ"* who definitely does not *"know God"* nor does he *"keep his commandments"* (1 John 2:3).

Warnings about Error and How to Deal with its Teachers

For many deceivers are gone forth into the world, even they that confess not that Jesus Christ cometh in the flesh. This is the deceiver and the antichrist (2 John 7, ASV). *Many deceivers, who do not acknowledge Jesus Christ as coming in the flesh, have gone out into the world. Any such person is the deceiver and the antichrist* (2 John 7, NIV).

To get a better understanding of *"the antichrist"* and his teachings read the introductory material on First John again. Give special attention to the explanations given in the commentary section of 1 John 2:18-27 and 4:1-6. The problems John's readers faced were compounded by the multitude of *"deceivers who are gone forth into the world."* *"Anti-christ"* is not limited to only one individual. John said, *"Even now have there arisen **many** antichrists"* (1 John 2:18) with just as many false teachings. To *"confess not"* is to openly deny the incarnation of Jesus. *"Cometh in the flesh,"* as a present active participle, insists that Christ's human nature is a continuing extension of His redemptive role. He is still *"man"* (cf. John 5:27; Acts 17:31; 1 Timothy 2:5).

The phrase *"gone forth (**exelthon** = exited) into the world"* may imply that they have left the church. The same verb and same tense is used in 1 John 2:19. Even if they have departed from the church, their doctrines of error are still a menace to the believers. They were still militantly bent on converting true believers to their views (cf. 1 John 2:26). Marcus Dodd remarks: "From their own point of view, they were Christian missionaries. From the standpoint of the Presbyter (John) they were impostors." Yet another commentator, Stott observes: "As the Apostles were sent forth into the world to preach the truth, so these false teachers had gone forth to teach lies, as emissaries of the devil, the father of lies." As traveling itinerants, they tried to avail themselves of the customary hospitality Christians gave to traveling preachers. John hastens to forewarn of the dangers they represent (cf. 2 John 8). He also wants to forbid Christians from any partnership with them in the spread of their error (cf. 2 John 9-10).

The phrase *"they confess not that Jesus Christ cometh in the flesh"* says their denial of the humanity of Jesus seems to be the most characteristic error they fostered (See comments on 1 John 4:3). The root background of their teaching lies in their view that flesh is intrinsically evil and spirit is good. Therefore, they are loathe to believe that Jesus as a representative of Spirit God would voluntarily take on human nature. For them he only "seemed" to have a fleshly body. Such a doctrine dismantles everything we know about the vicarious death of Jesus, His redemptive blood, and ultimately His glorious resurrection. John calls them *"the deceiver and the antichrist."*

*Look to yourselves, that ye lose not the things which **we*** *have wrought, but that ye receive a full reward* (2 John 8, ASV). *Watch out that you do not lose what you have worked for, but that you may be rewarded fully* (2 John 8, NIV).

The word *"look"* (***blepete***) is present active imperative and carries the impact of a warning to "look out!" The same verb is used by Jesus, when he warned his disciples about false teachers: *"Be on guard! Be alert!"* (***blepete***) (Mark 13:23). Could believers actually lose their souls by accepting false teaching? Absolutely! To *"receive the full reward"* is to inherit the eternal blessings God offers His people. To be able to   *"receive the full reward"* believers must not lose what they have worked for. The *"things we have wrought"* is the message the Apostles taught about Jesus and His mission of salvation. The *"we"* probably relates to the teaching work of the apostolic college and not to the labor of the believers. Paul frequently expressed his concern for doctrinal purity among those he taught. His *"I fear for you, that somehow I have wasted my efforts on you"* (Galatians 4:11; cf. 1 Thessalonians 3:5) motivated his admonition to the brethren. So John here insists again that the brethren *"See that what you have heard from the beginning remains in you . . . just as it has taught you, remain in him* (1 John 2:24, 27).

Whosoever goeth onward and abideth not in the teaching of Christ, hath not God; he that abideth in the teaching, the same hath the Father and the Son (2 John 9, ASV). *Anyone who runs ahead and does not continue in the teaching of Christ does not have God; whoever continues in the teaching has both the Father and the Son* (2 John 9, NIV).

The phrase *"Whosoever goeth onward"* (***Pas ho proagon*** = *"run* ahead <u>too far</u>" as the New English Bible translates) relates to any teacher who goes **beyond** the apostolic message. Possibly John is using gnostic claims that they have progressed beyond the "superficial" teachings of the Apostles as the Gnostic viewed their message. Anyone who goes beyond the Apostles message has actually departed from the message. Indeed, he *"abides not in the teachings of Christ."* Evidently John accuses these heretics of over stepping his message about Christ. Paul insisted, *"They will turn their ears away from the truth and turn aside **to myths**"* (2 Timothy 4:4). Teachers who leave behind apostolic truth have also left God behind because they do *"not have God."*

John properly refers to the message Christ continue to teach through His chosen spokesman with *"the teachings of (**tou** is genitive of possession) Christ."* The usage of the Greek requires that the genitive be interpreted **not** as objective as in "the teaching about Christ," but as subjective as in **"Christ's** teaching." Such a view blends in well with John's insistence that his readers should remain in the message they heard *"from the beginning."* (1 John 2:24). Certainly the impact of John's witness contained in his first epistle powerfully affirmed the human/divine/messiah personhood of Jesus.

The phrase *"whoever continues in the teaching"* accepts John's testimony as coming from God. It is therefore the truth and not a lie (cf. 1 John 2:21). The *"teaching"* is also a believer's all sufficient source for the truth. He does not need any other message or something different (cf. 1 John 2:27). It is the permanent, available origin of all teaching about Christ. It is *"the truth, which lives in us and will be with us **forever**"* (2 John 2).

The one who remains in this *"teaching of Christ. . . has both the Father and the Son"* — this phrase assures those who remain firmly planted in the *"truth"* that their relation with God and His Son is secure. No one can have the *"Father"* if he denies the *"Son."* The *"Son"* is both the revelation of the *"Father"* (cf. John 1:18) and also the only avenue to union with Him (cf. John 14:6). Peter affirms, *"**Through him** (Christ) you believe in God, . . . and so your faith and hope are in God"* (1 Peter 1:21).

If any one cometh unto you, and bringeth not this teaching, receive him not into your house, and give him no greeting (2 John 10, ASV). *"f anyone comes to you and does not bring this teaching, do not take him into your house or welcome him* (2 John 10, NIV).

As mentioned in the introduction to <u>Second John</u>, there were many itinerant teachers who traveled the roads of the Roman empire during the first century. And quite evidently not all of them were preachers of the truth. In his first epistle, the Apostle had imperatively imposed two obligations upon his readers. **First,** *"do not believe every spirit"* and **second,** *"test the spirits to see whether they are from God"* (1 John 4:1). In 2 John he gives guidelines to govern all cases when the *"teacher"* is tested and is a *"deceiver who has gone out into the world." "The deceiver"* must not be offered hospitality in the home, nor given an audience for his error, nor yet granted any affirmation of support when he leaves. Again with two imperatives, John insists: *"receive him not"* (**me-lambanete** = do not welcome) and *"give him no greetings"* (**melegete xairein** = do not salute him with favour).

John's order does not prohibit the casual invitation to a believer in error into one's home to explain *"to him the way of God more adequately"* (Acts 18:26). A. T. Robertson says, "When propagandists of error were carrying on regular campaigns to destroy loyalty to Christ as Lord and Savior, then they must be refused hospitality. . . . such would inevitably involve endorsement of their teaching and lives." Christians are not to allow false teachers to use their homes as a base of operation. When a person *"goes out into the world"* as a merchant of lies and he does not bring the teachings of truth, he must not be permitted to market his error from a true believer's home.

For he that giveth him greeting **partaketh** *in his evil works* (2 John 11, ASV) [Emphasis added]. *Anyone who welcomes him shares in his wicked work"* (2 John 11, NIV).

John says, *"For (**gar** = because) he that giveth him greeting"* (***xairein*** = hail) is aiding and abetting a doctrinal renegade. ***"Partaketh"*** (***koinonei*** = fellowships) means to share as a partner in the spread of the false teacher's heresy. That man's *"works"* are *"evil"* and it is equally *"evil"* to contribute to any cause inspired by Satan. His *"evil works"* (***ergois ponerois*** = works of depravity and iniquity) rooted in the doctrinally unsound arguments are destructive to a Christian's ultimate salvation. Jesus warned His disciples to be cautious of the Pharisees. He said, ***"'Leave them/aphete*** (let them alone, divorce, send away); *they are blind guides. If a blind man leads a blind man, both will fall into a pit'"* (Matthew 15:14). This command demands their isolation by refusing them a podium from which to peddle their perversions of truth. Jesus explained the rationale for His demand by saying that the blind leading the blind is dangerous.

> *Having many things to write unto you, I would not write them with paper and ink: but I hope to come unto you, and to speak face to face, that your joy may be made full* (2 John 12, ASV). *I have much to write to you, but I do not want to use paper and ink. Instead, I hope to visit you and talk with you face to face, so that our joy may be complete* (2 John 12, NIV).

John seems to be explaining the evident brevity of this letter. Apparently he expected to visit the church soon. *"Face to face"* (***stoma pros stoma*** = literally, mouth to mouth) is a much more practical form of communication. There are many negative trends that gnostic error could introduce into Christian thinking. John wishes to address these and other topics on a personal level. John reassures them of the sacred truths he taught them and reconfirms their confidence in their ultimate redemption in Christ — (In order/so that) *"**that** your joy may be made full.*

The children of thine elect sister salute thee (2 John 13, ASV). *The children of your chosen sister send their greetings* (2 John 13, NIV).

This is a characteristic salutation Apostles gave when they closed their letters to the churches. Inter-congregational fraternity was always remembered. Prayers of grace, love, mercy, and peace were always encouraged among the churches (Note specific occasions of such apostolic greetings in the following scriptures: Romans 16:5, 16; 1 Corinthians 16:19; 2 Corinthians 13:13; Philippians 4:21-22; Titus 3:15; Hebrews 13:24 and 1 Peter 5:13).

SPECIAL NOTE: Second John forcefully instructs Christians not to encourage, assist, or have fellowship in the spread of false teaching. Third John, with equal force, requires Christians to support, encourage, and welcome teachers of truth into their homes. It becomes imperative that Christians *"prove the spirits, whether they are of God"* (1 John 4:1, ASV). Such testing aids the decision about whom to support or not support when faced with a proven heretic.

The Third Epistle of John

INTRODUCTION

As was <u>Second John</u>, so <u>Third John</u> was written by *"the elder"* to a beloved disciple and friend named *"Gaius."* There is no salutation presented in the opening of this brief epistle unless verse 24 contains John's greeting. Even so, John's expressions are more a prayer for physical health and material prosperity for his friend. John is very vocal in his praise of the way Gaius consistently assists and supports missionaries of the message John preached. The Apostle is equally critical of *"Diotrephes,"* who consistently opposed any and all teachers of John's message.

<u>Second John</u> had cautioned Christians about extending hospitality, support, and encouragement to any false teacher. <u>Third John</u> seeks to establish the responsibility of all believers in their partnership with those who are preaching the truth. Biblical guidelines are found in this epistle that should govern members of the church in their participation in the mission assignment Christ gave His people. Faithful brethren *"ought"* (**opheilei** = duty bound) to support those who *"for the sake of the Name went forth, taking nothing of the Gentiles"* (3 John 7-8). For John, this is an important part of *"walking in the truth"* (3 John 4). Even if there are domineering personalities, such as Diotrephes, in the congregation that oppose the practice, Christians must not allow such opposition to deter them from their mission obligation. *"Demetrius"* is evidently a missionary approved by John and is probably the reason behind the writing of this letter. It seems that Diotrephes would have prohibited Gaius from offering hospitality

to Demetrius. So John sends instructions designed to compliment Gaius for his support of gospel preachers and to encourage him to persevere in the practice. This short letter is built around these three personalities: Gaius, Diotrephes, and Demetrius.

Who is Gaius?

Clearly the *"elder"* (**presbuteros** = an old man) is the Apostle John as he was also identified in the introduction to <u>Second John</u>. The specific identity of this Gaius cannot be definitely established. There are a number of men named Gaius recorded in the New Testament. Paul wrote the letter of Romans from Corinth probably composed in the home of one he called: *"Gaius, whose hospitality I and the whole church here enjoy send you his greetings"* (Romans 16:23). He is probably the same Gaius who is mentioned with Crispus as Corinthian believers Paul had personally baptized (cf. 1 Corinthians 1:14). There is another Gaius mentioned together with Aristarcus as *"Paul's traveling companions from Macedonia"* (cf. Acts 19:29). There is also *"Gaius of Derbe,"* who traveled with Paul, Timothy, and others to Troas. (cf. Acts 20:4). It is quite possible that the *"Gaius"* to whom John is writing is identified with any of the above.

However, there are a number of things we learn about this *"Gaius"* from the things John and others say about him. He is evidently a spiritually prosperous Christian, given John's evaluation in 3 John 2. Other brothers came to John to tell him about Gaius' *"faithfulness to the truth and how you continue to walk in the truth"* (3 John 3). He is involved in a *"faithful work"* of supporting foreign missionaries (cf. 3 John 5). The missionaries themselves *"have told the church about your love"* (3 John 6). John encourages him to *"show hospitality to such men so that we may work together for the truth"*(3 John 8). John encourages him to imitate good and avoid evil (cf. 3 John 11).

Hospitality and Mission Awareness Commended

3 John 1-4

The elder unto Gaius the beloved, whom I love in truth
(3 John 1, ASV). *The elder to my dear friend Gaius,*
whom I love in the truth (3 John 1, NIV).

Gaius may have been a member of the church to whom John
wrote his second epistle. At least that could be surmised from
John's statement, *"I wrote to the church, but Diotrephes, who*
loves to be first, will have nothing to do with us" (3 John 9). In that
correspondence he had cautioned the brethren against aiding false
teachers in the spread of their error. John clarified the matter in
detail in this epistle so that the brethren would not become too
cautious and fail to support any teachers. He is intent on
maintaining the practice of support when the messenger is a proven
spokesman for God. The mission enterprise initiated under the
Great Commission must continue undiminished by dictatorial
leaders in the church.

John's love for Gaius probably grew out of his appreciation
for the way Gaius supports and encourages mission work. John's
love is *"in truth,"* meaning it is genuine. *"Love"* and *"truth"* are
twin companions of the cause of Christ. Four times the word
"beloved" is used in this brief letter to show John's sincere
devotion to Gaius (cf. 3 John 1, 2, 5, 11). In the three Johannine
epistles the Apostle used this word *"beloved"* (**agapetos** = well
loved, dear friend) at least ten times.

Beloved, I pray that in all things thou mayest prosper and
be in health; even as thy soul prospereth (3 John 2,
ASV). *Dear friend, I pray that you may enjoy good*
health and that all may go well with you, even as your
soul is getting along well (3 John 2, NIV).

The word *"prosper"* (***euodousthai*** = to grant a successful issue) in John's prayer for Gaius seems to imply a request for financial affluence. Since John was aware of how Gaius used his wealth to support missionaries, this was an appropriate request for which to pray. *"Even as your soul prospers"* (***euodein*** = well being) became the measure of John's request for the material well-being of Gaius. Such an affirmation shows John's confidence that Gaius was spiritually prosperous. How many brethren do we know for whom we could only wish that they were as spiritually healthy as they are financially rich?

The phrase *"and be in health"* (***hygiainein*** = fit and well, cf. Luke 5:31) deals with the physical well-being of Gaius. The same standard of *"as your soul prospers"* applies to the soundness of this brother's body. It is right and wholesome that Christians seek God's blessings, both fiscal and physical, for those who generously sustain the work of the Lord with their resources. Moses said, *"Remember the LORD your God, for it is he who gives you the ability to produce wealth"* (Deuteronomy 8:18).

Paul said,

> *Now he* (God) *who supplies seed to the sower and bread for food will also supply and increase your store of seed and will enlarge the harvest of your righteousness* (2 Corinthians 9:10).

> ***For*** [emphasis added] *I rejoice greatly, when brethren came and bare witness unto thy truth, even as thou walkest in truth"* (3 John 3, ASV). *It gave me great joy to have some brothers come and tell about your faithfulness to the truth and how you continue to walk in the truth* (3 John 3, NIV).

The word *"For"* (***gar*** = because) becomes the ground from which the previous statement was made. The spiritual prosperity of Gaius was evidenced by his *"walk in the truth."* Brethren who had recently visited with Gaius made a report to John that caused the Apostle to *"rejoice greatly."* John notes that it is *"your love"* which indicates that he had embraced the truth and held it as his own possession. To *"walk in truth"* demands that the Word of God is not simply a doctrine to be believed, but it demands a lifestyle consistent with the doctrine believed.

> *Greater joy have I none than this, to hear of my children walking in the truth* (3 John 4, ASV). *I have no greater joy than to hear that my children are walking in the truth* (3 John 4, NIV).

It seems evident that Gaius was one of John's converts. Therefore, John's greatest *"joy"* comes from news of the fidelity of one whom he led to Christ. This is almost a verbatim repetition of his statement to the *"Elect Lady and her children"* (2 John 4). Paul expressed the same intense personal joy about those he had converted. He wrote, *"Therefore, my brothers, you whom I love and long for, my joy and crown, that is how you should stand firm in the Lord, dear friends"* (Philippians 4:1). He also wrote, *"For what is our hope, our joy, or the crown in which we will glory in the presence of our Lord Jesus when he comes? Is it not you? Indeed, you are our glory and joy"* (1 Thessalonians 3:5). There would be few sorrows more tragic for any missionary (as Paul) to have *"run my races in vain"* (Galatians 2:2) or to see that *"our efforts might have been useless"* for some church (1 Thessalonians 3:5).

3 John 5-14

Beloved, thou doest a faithful work in whatsoever thou doest toward them that are brethren and strangers withal

(3 John 5, ASV). *Dear friend, you are faithful in what you are doing for the brothers, even though they are strangers to you* (3 John 5, NIV).

A *"faithful work"* not only indicates that Gaius faithfully engaged in the *"work,"* but also that it is a *"work"* in which he strongly believes. He knew the redemptive purposes the *"work"* promoted and he believed in its ultimate success. The *"whatsoever thou doest"* will be defined in the next three verses. It involves the financial support of Gospel missionaries. Those *"brethren"* were foreigners, as indicated by the term *"strangers"* (**xenos** = expatriots). The fact that they were preachers traveling to spread the Gospel is affirmed by John's charge to *"set them forward on their journey"* (3 John 6).

Offering hospitality to traveling *"brethren"* was an often repeated command to Christians (cf. Heb.13:2; 1 Timothy 3:2; 1 Peter 4:9). It would be good for the reader of this commentary to look at the discussion about The Practice Of Christian Hospitality in the introduction to 2 John. Gaius was a sterling example of such an open-door policy toward teachers of the truth.

Who bare witness to thy love before the church: whom thou wilt do well to set forward on their journey worthily of God (3 John 6, ASV). *They have told the church about your love. You will do well to send them on their way in a manner worthy of God* (3 John 6, NIV).

The missionaries who were received into the home of Gaius were generous in publicizing the hospitality of John's *"beloved"* disciple. They *"bare witness"* to the hospitality Gaius offered them which is a true expression of *"love"* for them and for the work they were promoting.

This disciple may or may not be the same Gaius whom Paul mentioned in his Roman letter. Paul wrote about a Gaius who was his host (cf. Romans 16:23). At least the Corinthian Gaius had the same hospitable practice as this one about whom John wrote.

The phrase *"whom thou wilt do well* (**kalos** = a beautiful thing) *"to set forward"* (**propempein** = to propel) *on their journey"* is probably referring to Jesus' Great Commission (cf. Matthew 28:19-20; Mark 16:15-15). The church in New Testament times probably did not refer to Christ's universal assignment as the "Great Commission," as we do. If they had a term by which to designate that mandate, it would probably have been called the **"Great Propelling."** That is the impact the words *"set forward"* contain. The verb *"set forward"* is used in the following verses: Acts 15:3; Acts 20:38; Acts 21:5; Romans 15:24; 1 Corinthians 16:6, 10; 2 Corinthians 1:16 and Titus 3:13.

To *"set forward,"* according to the dictionary means to help on one's journey with food, money, by arranging for companions, means of travel, etc. It means to supply all the things that are necessary to the success of the mission and for the needs of the missionary. Paul used that same verb (**propempein**) when he instructed Titus, *"Set forward/do everything you can to help Zenas the lawyer and Apollos on their way and see that they have everything they need"* (Titus 3:13). Titus was to see to their needs in such a way that *"nothing be wanting."* Their mission was preaching the gospel to the lost. They must not be deterred because of a lack of financial resources. Then Paul added this injunction for the church, *"Our people must learn to devote themselves to doing what is good, in order that they may provide for daily necessities and not live unproductive lives"* (Titus 3:14). The practice of supporting missionaries must be *"maintained"* with *"diligence"* (**spoudais** = speedily). After all, the church had been taught the Gospel, and Paul imperatively commanded, *"Let him that is taught in the word communicate* (**koinoneito** = contribute) *unto him that teacheth in all good things"* (Galatians 6:6, ASV). These were all responsibilities Gaius had learned well and faithfully practiced.

The phrase *"worthily* (**axios** = befitting, of like value) *of God"* is an adverb of manner. It defines the religious devotion God deserves. This phrase insists that missionaries of truth must be treated with the same kind of value as God Himself. The Lord often taught His representatives, *"He who receives you receives me, and he who receives me receives the one who sent me"* (Matthew 10:40).

Because that for the sake of the Name they went forth taking nothing of the gentiles (3 John 7, ASV). *It was for the sake of the Name that they went out, receiving no help from the pagans* (3 John 7, NIV).

Christians *"will do well"* to support missionaries of the Gospel. *"For the sake of the Name"* defines the nature and purpose of their mission. The *"Name"* is used often in the New Testament to identify the **cause** of Christ. *"For his name's sake"* defined Paul's mission *"among all the nations"* (Romans 1:5). The early church was described as *"rejoicing because they had been counted worthy of suffering disgrace for the Name"* (Acts 5:41). The mission of those whom Gaius assisted was to publicize *"the Name"* through whom alone is God's offer of salvation (cf. Acts 4:12).

The phrase *"receiving no help from the pagans/gentiles"* declares the restricted sources from whom mission personnel were to receive support. It was not, and still is not, the duty of the those who are part of the *"spirit of error"* to support the spread of the message of salvation. That is a task God has placed on the shoulders of the church. The *"Gentiles"* (***ethnikoi*** = heathens or pagans RSV/NIV) stand in contrast with the believers. There does not seem to be a prohibition to accept gifts from the unconverted. It rather seems clear that those evangelists did not solicit contributions from non-believers.

*We therefore **ought** to welcome such, that we may be*

fellow-workers for the truth (3 John 8, ASV) [Emphasis added]. *"We ought therefore to show hospitality to such men so that we may work together for the truth* (3 John 8, NIV).

In contrast to the unbelievers who do not support itinerant evangelists, *"we"* (Christians) must do so. *"Ought"* (***opheilomen*** = duty bound, indebted) insists that believers have a moral obligation to offer hospitality when the missionary comes and to support him when he goes forth. It is good to recall that these two assignments, receiving and sending forth or supporting, are prohibited to the Christian if the teacher is not true to the apostolic message (cf. 2 John 9-10).

The phrase *"fellow-workers for the truth"* means that the missionary and those who support him are colleagues in a common cause. Their partnership in the spread of the *"Name"* gains for both the "sender" and the "sent" the title of *"fellow-workers of God"* (cf. 1 Corinthians 3:9; 2 Corinthians 6:1). Titus was told by Paul to see that *"our people learn to maintain good works for necessary uses, that they be not unfruitful"* (Titus 3:14, ASV). The *"necessary uses"* relates to the missionary's needs. The church that does not involve itself in spreading the Gospel beyond itself is *"unfruitful"* in a most urgent cause! To be *"unfruitful"* is the direct opposite to being *"fellow-workers for the truth."*

I wrote somewhat unto the church: but Diotrephes, who loveth to have the preeminence among them, receiveth us not (3 John 9, ASV). *I wrote to the church, but Diotrephes, who loves to be first, will have nothing to do with us* (3 John 9, NIV).

The practice of "receiving" and "supporting" traveling preachers is all the more imperative when domineering personalities like Diotrephes want to impose restrictions. In practice and in motivation Gaius and Diotrephes were vastly different. Gaius walked in the truth, welcomed the brethren, and supported preachers of the truth. Diotrephes was not only full of personal pride (*"loved preeminence"*) but was also ambitious to rule the congregation. It may be that both men were members of the same church.

The phrase *"I wrote somewhat unto the church"* may refer to John's second epistle. If that is the case, then John had instructed the church not to extend assistance to any who did was not following the teachings of Christ (cf. 2 John 9). And if that was the case, *"Diotrephes received us not."* He did not acknowledge John's apostolic authority. His rejection of John's letter may have come from his desire for prominence in the church. Or it may have been rooted in the doctrinal positions he held that were contrary to John's teaching. It is quite possible that Diotrephes subscribed to some gnostic theology that caused him to oppose John. That would explain why he refused to allow members of the congregation to *"receive the brethren"* (missionaries) and even threatened to *"cast out of the church"* anyone who helped them (cf. 3 John 10). Social prestige, personal ambition, and doctrinal deviation seems to explain his behavior. The bottom line is that his problem was moral, because his actions were sinful — there is no other explanation.

*Therefore, if I come, I will bring to remembrance his works which he doeth, **prating against us** with wicked words; and not content therewith, neither doth he himself receive the brethren, and them that would he forbiddeth and casteth them out of the church* (3 John 10, ASV) [emphasis added]. *So if I come, I will call attention to what he is doing, gossiping maliciously about us. Not satisfied with that, he refuses to welcome the brothers. He also stops those who want to do so and puts them out of the church* (3 John 10, NIV).

John switched from the singular pronoun *"I wrote"* to the plural *"us"* in 3 John 9, then back to the singular *"if I come,"* and then to *"us"* in 3 John 10. John may be speaking of the collective authority of the apostolic college. He was aware that he had the authority to issue commands which he expected the church to obey. But Diotrephes was not willing to accept John's authority. He authenticated himself and even sought to excommunicate anyone who resisted him.

The phrase *"if I come"* may be a word of warning to Diotrephes. John then would have occasion to confront him. It would be easy for John to expose his works as abusive in the church. John describes him as *"prating against us* (**phlyaron** = talking nonsense, bringing unjustified charges) *with wicked words"* (**pornerois** = evil). *"Prating"* is translated with the word *"gossip"* (NIV) and *"tattlers"* (ASV) in 1 Timothy 5:13. Alexander Ross comments that these are not simply "words of an empty windbag; they were **wicked words**, perniciously evil words." This is the same *"evil"* as John used in reference to Cain (cf. 1 John 3:12) and to the Devil (cf. 1 John 5:18-19).

Evidently Diotrephes not only rejected John's apostolic authority, he accused him of unjustified intrusion into "his" church. He may have even charged him with teaching false doctrine! R. W. Stott states that Diotrephes "evidently regarded John as a dangerous rival to his own assumed authority in the church and sought to undermine his position by slanderous gossip. He was not satisfied with a campaign of malicious gossip about John, but went further and deliberately defied 'the elder.'"

The fact that Diotrephes *"refuses to welcome brothers"* shows his aversion either to the men or to their teaching. He offered no hospitality to evangelists of the truth. His hostility further expressed itself by his efforts to *"put them out of the church"* those who wanted to be partners with the evangelists. His use of tyrannical power must be what John was referring to when he spoke of *"his evil works which he doeth."*

Beloved, imitate not that which is evil, but that which is good. He that doeth good is of God: he that doeth evil hath not seen God (3 John 11, ASV). *Dear friend, do not imitate what is evil but what is good. Anyone who does what is good is from God. Anyone who does what is evil has not seen God* (3 John 11, NIV).

Having denounced the evil works of Diotrephes, John again writes to encourage Gaius not to *"imitate (**mimou** = to mimic) what is evil."* From John's perspective the actions of Diotrephes may preclude him from being a faithful Christian. In John's first epistle he strongly affirmed that *"whosoever sinneth hath not seen him* (God) *or knoweth him"* (God) (1 John 3:6). He hastens to add that *"he that doeth sin is of the devil"* (1 John 3:8). The *"works which he doeth"* (present active indicative) (cf. 3 John 10) signal a settled practice of unholy opposition to John. In this verse, *"he that doeth evil"* (present active participle) defines the career of Diotrephes. Serious doubt could be cast about that man's fellowship with God. When John said that a habitual sinner *"hath not seen God or knoweth him,"* he thus excludes the possibility that such a man was ever genuinely converted to Christ. Such preclusive language by John in these epistles generally was addressed toward confirmed Gnostics. Conversely, *"he that doeth good is of God,"* as was Gaius, and possibly Demetrius who is mentioned in the next verse.

Demetrius hath the witness of all men, and of the truth itself: yea, we also bear witness, and thou knowest that our witness is true (3 John 12, ASV). *Demetrius is well spoken of by everyone — and even by the truth itself. We also speak well of him, and you know that our testimony is true* (3 John 12, NIV).

Demetrius was probably the unconscious subject of the

conflict between Gaius and Diotrephes. In the context it would appear that Gaius wanted to offer hospitality and support to Demetrius, but Diotrephes strongly opposed such an alliance. The phrase *"Demetrius is well spoken of by everyone"* affirms his loyalty to the truth John taught. It may also insist that he was consistently practicing the truth and actively spreading the Gospel message. Even John placed his stamp of approval on this worthy evangelist. John would not lie about such a critical matter — *"and you know that our testimony is true."*

> *I had many things to write unto thee, but I am unwilling to write them to thee with ink and pen* (3 John 13, ASV). *I have much to write to you, but I do not want to do so with pen and ink* (3 John 13, NIV).

John's final words to Gaius are almost a verbatim repetition of John's conclusion in <u>Second John</u>. There he did not want to *"write with paper and ink"* while here he does not want to communicate *"with ink and pen."* It would have been interesting to hear John discuss verbally the *"many things"* he wanted to talk about with Gaius. We will just have to be content with what we have.

> *But I hope shortly to see thee, and we shall speak face to face. Peace be unto thee. The friends salute thee. Salute the friends by name* (3 John 14, ASV). *I hope to see you soon, and we will talk face to face. Peace to you. The friends here send their greetings. Greet the friends there by name* (3 John 14, NIV)

Being *"face to face"* (**stoma pros stoma** = literally mouth to mouth) with Gaius is a more congenial format for the *"things"* John wants to discuss.

John closes his letter invoking God's blessings on his

"beloved friend." "Friend" is a very good title for brethren who love one another. Jesus referred to *"our friend Lazarus"* (John 11:11). He told the disciples *"you are my friends, if ye do the things that I command you"* (John 15:14). In that same context Jesus added: *"No longer do I call you servants...but I have called you friends"* (John 15:15).

The phrase *"Salute the friends by name"* seems to mean that Gaius should greet them name by name — salute each one of them.

APPLICATION

There are few passages in the New Testament that more clearly present the principles that must direct the church's evangelistic mission. The *"setting forward"* of mission personnel is not optional to God's people. The urgency contained in John's *"ought"* (*opheilei* = duty bound) is filled with greater moral obligation than the word normally suggests to us. Anyone who would prohibit, hinder, or in any way discourage any aspiring missionary is really playing into the hands of the Devil and all his cohorts like Diotrephes. The fervency of a brother like Gaius deserves to be imitated. May his tribe increase!

May God continue to bless you as you continue your study of the Epistles of John.

Gerald Paden
Sunset International Bible Institute
Lubbock, Texas

Bibliography

Ante-Nicene Fathers, Vol.5, pg.58,
     (Wm.B. Eerdmans, 1967)
Barclay, William, *The Letters of John and Jude,*
     The Daily Study Bible (St. Andrew Press, 1976)
Brooke, A.E., *Commentary on the Johanine Epistles,*
     The International Critical Commentary (T. & T. Clark,
     1912)
Bruce, F.F., *The epistles of John,*
     (Pickering & Inglis), 1978)
Dobbs, C.H., Commentary on the Johanine Epistles,
     Moffatt New Testament Commentary (Hodder &
     Stoughton, 1946).
Nicoll, W. Robertson, *The epistles of St. John,*
     The Expositor's Bible, (Geo. H. Doran).
Roberts, J.W., *The Letters of John,*
     (R.B. Sweet, 1969)
Robertson, A.T., *Word Pictures in the New Testament,*
     New York & London, 1931.
Ross, Alexander, *The Epistles of James and John,*
     (Eerdmans Pub. Co. 1970)
Wescott, B.F., *Commentary on the Epistles of St. John,*
     (Eerdmans, 1966).

Printed in the United States
75143LV00004B/121-219

9 780975 518397